The Gift of Jazzy

CINDY ADAMS

The Gift of Jazzy

ST. MARTIN'S PRESS

NEW YORK

www.stmartins.com

Design by Kathryn Parise

LIBRARY OF CONGRESS CATALOGING-IN-PUBLICATION DATA
Adams, Cindy Heller.
    The gift of Jazzy / Cindy Adams.—1st ed.
        p. cm.
    ISBN 0-312-27307-X
    1. Adams, Cindy Heller. 2. Gossip columnists—United States—
Biography. I. Title.

PN4874.A27 A3 2003
070.4'44—dc21

2002073973

First Edition: February 2003

10 9 8 7 6 5 4 3 2 1

To Joey and Jessie,
whom I will always love with my whole heart.
Wherever you are I hope you're smiling.

AUTHOR'S NOTE

The stories in this book roughly encompass the year following my husband's, Joey's, death in December 1999. I have taken a few very tiny editorial liberties with the time line in the interests of flow, readability, and, of course, humor. However, this account is true to the spirit of my experience during that year of change and renewal.

CONTENTS

1. My Joey   1
2. Jazzy   15
3. Call Me Mommy   29
4. Our First Christmas   39
5. Bed Luck   51
6. It's a Dog's Life   63
7. Trainer Hell   73
8. Mother's Day   87
9. A Day at the *NYP*   101
10. The Dirty Dog   115
11. Don't Fence Me In   121
12. On the Road   135
13. The Apartment   153
14. Prince Jazzy   165
15. Shoe Business   179
16. Sibling Rivalry   191

17.   Jazzy's Phone Fetish   207
18.   Thanksgiving   221
19.   Romeo and Jazzyet   227
20.   Big Women, Little Dogs   239
21.   Together Forever   249
      A Final Word   257

The Gift of
Jazzy

CHAPTER 1

My Joey

Joey and I had been together forever. I almost can't remember a time I wasn't with him. I think I came out of the womb married. Instead of a teething ring, I had a wedding ring. We were married when I was sixteen.

In his golden days he'd say, "Cindy and I became man and wife so long ago, Moses himself performed the ceremony. Our license is on a stone tablet."

My husband did everything for me. The only thing he ever did *to* me was grow old. And so, in the winter of his life, I did for him.

※

Age is a bitch. Worse than a mugger in a dark alley, because age brings a slow death. Minute by minute, inch by inch, here a little, there a little, year by year by year. Age robs you of your dignity, ability, agility, memory, self-respect. It forces once-powerful somebodies to beg favors from nobodies.

It humiliates. It debilitates. It assassinates.

In the old days, comedian Joey Adams was a big-time pro headlining those Broadway movie theaters that are now long gone. Glossy palaces like the Paramount, the State, the Capitol, the Roxy. He and his friends and colleagues—Frank Sinatra, Johnnie Ray, Guy Lombardo (all of whom are also gone)—did six a day then. Six stage shows to go along with each showing of the movie.

I was a teenage model when Joey and I were wed. Why did I marry someone so senior? Because Joey loved me the same way my mother did. Without reservation. Some brides are motivated by passion, money, companionship. For me, the man I married was an extension of the life I'd had. If I got a cold, Joey sneezed. I felt safe.

The man who swore to take care of me was successful and, to my mind, sophisticated. Attractive in a non-pretty-boy way. Sharp looking. Beige cashmere coats. Snap-brim fedoras. Custom shirts with starched French cuffs. Diamond studs with the tux.

He lived big. Cadillac Eldorado convertible. Home was the Waldorf Towers. With Joey, I began to socialize with the famous. I'd been to people's houses before, but now the houses I was going to belonged to people like Bob Hope. Joey took me to Bob's Palm Springs estate. Bob gave me a "Hiya, honey," then showed me through the enormous closet that housed just his golf clothes. "My Lord," I gasped. "There must be a hundred pairs of pants hanging in one row." "Naaaah," said Bob. "Only seventy."

Not exactly the type of conversation I'd been having at my mom's kitchen table. It was heady. Open Sesame to a world about which a young nobody could only have dreamt.

Joey knew everyone. Other young girls I knew were marrying boys their age and struggling to find their way. It was all babies, bills, infidelity. To me those bonds of eternal romantic passion seemed the illusion, while the richness of my life was the reality. An average night out for us was a black-tie event.

My husband gave me entrée to everybody and everything. I started in the gossip business by interviewing his friends. I'd graduated to $200-a-story articles for *TV Guide* and was working for the North American Newspaper Alliance around the time President John F. Kennedy summoned Joey. Joey was then president of the American

Guild of Variety Artists, to which all performers from Elvis to circus clowns belonged. In his dual role of quasi-political figure and performer, Joey became an ambassador in greasepaint. He was sent to head the first cultural exchange unit to Southeast Asia.

I hadn't been a bride for too many years when we started off on this four-month journey. Among those I interviewed on our expedition was Sukarno, who was then president of Indonesia. I wasn't too conversant with Indonesia. All I knew was you get to Beirut and make a right. Until then I'd been specializing in such hard-hitting, thought-provoking, incisive, in-depth think pieces as "Where Does Laurence Welk Go from Here?"

Sukarno liked the piece I wrote about him, and I was invited to return the following year to write his life story. *Sukarno: An Autobiography—As Told to Cindy Adams* was my first book, published in 1963. It sold all over the world, was translated into a dozen languages, and landed me a news commentator job on ABC-TV. Another I spoke with on this tour was the Shah of Iran. Over the years we met repeatedly in Iran and the United States, and I interviewed him and the empress extensively.

My husband gave me my career. And then he stepped back and watched me go. Joey allowed me to flourish, and I bloomed in the sunlight of his love.

I carried that aura into my writing. Joey's professional take-no-prisoners attitude formulated my own. Early on I complained, "Syndicates want me to tone down, soften the style so the column can travel. They say readers in Iowa or Utah won't get my edginess."

Said Joey, "Listen, even though she lived in the White House, Teddy Roosevelt's daughter Alice Roosevelt Longworth used to tell visitors, 'If you haven't got anything good to say about anyone, come sit by me.' So, frig 'em all. Be New York. The whole rest of the world is Bridgeport."

But that was a long time back. By the 1990s, Joey's glory days were over. Joey was no longer the guy with the smarts. No longer the hotshot entertainer who at a Friars Roast could say to Dean Martin, "Pal, if your zipper could only talk." And I, for sure, was no longer that girl with the baby-fat face who'd just won the title Miss Bagel.

Although I never thought about it in those early days, I guess down deep I knew that someday I'd have to pay back. But out of forty years, more than thirty of them were great. Most marriages are 50-50. Mine was 75-25. All the man ever wanted from me was to be number one in my heart. He treasured me. All he ever asked for was to be treasured by me.

And so, in the last half dozen years, I gave him not only what he wanted but also what he needed. I put my

own life on hold to take care of his. He did for me in the beginning. I did for him in the end. As my grandmother used to say, "The wheel turns."

But I don't say it wasn't tough. It was tough.

When Joey first started taking me around, he was New York's toastmaster-in-residence. Every dais. Every event. At one time if you ate a grapefruit in a Manhattan ball-room, it came with Joey. As he put it, "I've been around so long, been to so many dinners, I think if you take an enlargement of *The Last Supper* I'm third from the right."

And then came the first time he was invited to some major event but not asked to emcee. And then came the first time he was not even invited to the major event because the invitation came marked, "Mrs. Cindy Adams." And then came the first time he didn't even have the energy to accompany me to the major event.

Inside the witchy, bitchy gossip columnist who delivers six columns a week for the *New York Post* lived this secret agent. A player on two stages. One role being to spit on the mascara and sally forth reporting on openings and parties. The other to live among bedpans, to spend a sleepless night changing the sheets on a home hospital bed, to struggle lifting a 175-pound man who'd slipped out of my arms onto the floor.

My whole life changed as my husband changed. Our

whole lifestyle revolved on the changing Joey. When Joey and I had first moved into our apartment, the decor was attractive enough to have been featured in a *House and Garden* layout. But that soon changed as Joey's needs changed. Our library doorway had to be widened to make it wheelchair-accessible. That tore apart walls and ceilings. Then the floor had to be ripped up to anchor a grab bar so Joey could hoist himself up from his favorite armchair. I had to add a throw blanket to tuck around his legs, an egg-crate cushion to avoid bedsores, a footstool. I had to construct shelves and install cabinets so there could be a small heater, cubbyholes for medications, and whatever else had to be right at hand if needed.

The Ming table at his right elbow was configured to hold a box of Kleenex, cough drops, Vaseline because his lips and nose were always dry, a bell he could ring, and a baby monitor so he could be heard if whoever was watching him slipped out for a moment.

Since the library still needed to function as the setting for my own business meetings, I tried to prevent it taking on the look of an ICU. An identical slipcover was added to the armchair to circumvent the effects of spillage. Some supplies were hidden in an antique chest. A microwave was built inside an armoire, which precluded the need to cross the entire house when he wanted something warmed up. An enormous clock with oversize black numbers was screwed into the side of a couch so that Joey didn't have to raise his head to learn the time.

He always asked the time. Every ten minutes he'd ask the time. Without dates or appointments on which to base a day's schedule, time becomes something amorphous, free-floating. There's nothing to pinpoint. Hours become days, and days become lost.

After all the effort involved in furnishing this room, it still really wasn't working for Joey. The room opened to a terrace. Too quiet. No action. Hustle and bustle was in the other part of the apartment—in the kitchen. So I made our kitchen the center of life. An architect melded it into what was once a rear terrace. I had it glass enclosed so that the room became a large lounge and solarium. Big, comfy, overstuffed armchairs. Heated tile floor. Giant TV. Stands for Joey's favorite felt-tip pens. Racks for the large-print crossword puzzles he seemed no longer to be doing but I hoped he'd do again. Outlets nearby so we could plug in a turntable, so he could play and replay his comedy albums. Breakfast table and banquette for eight. This way, if I was out, he'd be in the midst of whatever was happening. Where food was being cooked, ironing was being done, deliveries were being made. He'd be able to experience whatever life was unfolding inside his shrunken world.

In that gray era when Joey was still going out some evenings for dinner, a problem was clothing. How to get new suits? The old ones were overly cleaned and getting shiny. They looked like mohair even though they were wool. Not only that, but he'd lost so much weight they didn't fit. There was one afternoon Joey was being taken to a neighborhood coffee shop where he occasionally enjoyed lunch. We walked him, me holding one arm, a friend holding the other, from the car straight into the coffee shop. His trousers fell down right in the street. The following night he was going to Le Cirque with his old friend Anthony Quinn. I don't remember Quinn's outfit, but I remember Joey's. The pants of his $2,500 suit featured a big diaper pin in back.

And there were other humiliations. The evening our car stopped at a service station. Joey in the back. Dozing. His head down on his Hermès tie. And the tie stained because when the hand becomes unsteady, the battle to keep oneself unspotted is a losing one. A balding, elderly passenger in another car sees him. Her dentures were out. And she says to my husband, "Joey Adams! How did you let yourself get like that?"

Besides his seven-day-a-week "Strictly for Laughs" column in the *New York Post*, Joey wrote books, magazine pieces, and material for politicians and lawyers who were making speeches. In addition to the *Post*, he had longtime contracts with other publications. Even when he could no longer remember people's names he could always remember jokes. Stick a needle in the man and he would spurt one-liners.

In his wind-down months, one of his magazine deals was canceled. The doctors had by then told me they'd given him three months. They undershot the estimate by four weeks.

He was in the countdown. I would've killed to keep him happy. I could not bear to see him hurt. I've long been in the business of doing favors and I'm not used to asking for them. It took a lot, but I called and pleaded for this one publication not to cancel his column. Even if they didn't think the output was as sharply edged as it used to be, I was just asking for another few months.

They refused.

Do I blame them? Not really. Will I forgive them? Not ever. Will I get them someday? I'll sure as hell try.

We tried to maintain whatever semblance of normal life we could. I'd take him out as much as possible. It was difficult. Besides physical deterioration there was mental confusion. He needed to know exactly, but exactly, where he was going. We tried to keep to whatever locations were familiar, except that they were no longer familiar.

A typical conversation as we set forth one evening: "Honey, we're going to your favorite Italian restaurant, Patsy's."

"Where is Patsy's?"

"You've been going to this same place for thirty-five years. Your picture's up on the wall. You know Patsy's."

"I know that I know Patsy's. What are you telling me about Patsy's for? Of course I know Patsy's. Where is it?"

"On Fifty-sixth Street, between Broadway and Eighth Avenue. Where it's always been. Same spot it's been since Sinatra first took you there."

"Please, you telling me about Patsy's? You kidding? I've gone to Patsy's all my life. Which side of the street is it on?"

"What do you mean, which side of the street?"

"What do you mean, what do I mean? Right or left?"

"It's a one-way street. It's on the right."

"Ground floor?"

The first few times I thought he was putting me on. Then I became irritated. Finally I realized the demon that now inhabited this man I'd known practically all my life no longer knew where Patsy's was. My husband had traversed the Great Divide. There was no pulling him back.

In the end fear was my constant companion. While I

was consciously busy handling whatever was immediate—another nurse, an ambulette, a pharmacy that wouldn't send urgently needed medication because the prescription couldn't be renewed and his doctor was traveling—what I couldn't handle consciously was the unconscious fear. The what ifs.

What if something happens at home suddenly and we can't handle it? What if he has to make another trip to the emergency room and it's the middle of the night? I have no brothers, no sisters, no family. Whom do I call? What if the hospital insists on measures with which I disagree?

And then came the night his breathing stopped for a few seconds. Fingers and lips turned blue. A longtime friend and Methodist minister, David Randolph, had come over to share dinner with us. We held hands at the bedside. We prayed. Joey's breath returned. But the Gray Specter was now the Unseen Guest in the house.

It was three weeks later. Riding inside the ambulance, these words from Jeremiah, Chapter 6, verse 14, rattled around my brain: "Peace, peace; when there is no peace."

It was two days later. December 2, 1999. I was the only one alive who knew Joey had gone. I was in his room in St. Vincent's Hospital. Alone. Stroking his face. He looked the same, his breathing under the oxygen mask appeared the same, but I divined something. What, I didn't know. The nurse, right outside the door, said, "I think you should say good-bye to him."

Then his doctors stepped in and said, "He's going."

I knew the last sense to leave is hearing. So I bent down and told the man I'd been with for more than forty years, "I love you, baby."

And then they told me, "He's gone." I literally handed him over to God.

Joey was gone. Now what was I going to do?

The answer was licking my toe.

CHAPTER 2

Jazzy

I t was a cold day. It was December 9. Indoors it was just as bitter. It was exactly one week to the day since my husband had died.

My home was filled with lawyers telling me that probate would take two years. A real estate broker had sent a note asking was I interested in selling my apartment since it might now seem too large and expensive for me to keep. My accountant was on the phone giving me the news that I had somehow acquired a tax audit for the two previous years.

And into this chilly atmosphere a warm puppy was suddenly thrust into my arms.

For too long I had known only an ailing, aging spouse. Life for me was strictly home health-care attendants, relief weekend nurses, rotating aides on an overnight shift. It was schedules for the medications, emergency numbers for the doctors, and prescriptions for the drugstore.

I could not have been less prepared for what happened that day. I wasn't used to any live thing growing in my house. No kids, no plants, no dogs. Definitely not some squirming, squiggling, squawling Yorkie who weighed two pounds, two ounces, and was the size of a rat's ass.

Neither of us seemed overly happy. For sure this unnecessary, unrequested hair ball wasn't all that thrilled to meet me, either. It wanted its mother, and the only resemblance possibly was my eensy amount of unwaxed facial hair and the fact that I polish off every table scrap I see. But even at three months of age this thing had no difficulty realizing I wasn't its mom.

Inside a Park Avenue kitchen with twelve unblinking eyes staring at it and with its head pressed hard against a scratchy sweater with clunky wood-block buttons wasn't where the creature wanted to be. It was like a surgeon's hand had just wrenched this little being from the womb and given her a slap. She was yowling that loud.

After years of terminal hibernation, my maternal instincts did not instantly kick in.

I was terrified. I was irritated. I was unsettled. The yapping was ceaseless. My problems seemed endless. And now, what to do with this wriggly, hairy mass? I didn't know. I didn't know how to hold it still. In fact, I didn't know how to hold it at all. One tiny hind leg the size of a chicken drumstick was bunched up in my right hand, its companion leg was out and flailing.

And six people were standing around frozen. Mouths open, eyes wide. They weren't sure what to do. They weren't sure what I would do. I wasn't sure what to do.

But all of a sudden, one of the bodies in that room instinctively knew for sure what to do. And did it. And right away a warm feeling came over me. The newest member of my household had just peed on me.

The fifteen-second silence felt like a full five minutes. Then came the first voice. "I guess we know how she feels about being here. She was pissed off," said the lawyer.

"Hey, that's good luck." His young assistant laughed nervously.

"No, you idiot, that's when you spill champagne," said the lawyer.

Joey, who wrote thirty-six joke books in his lifetime, used to tell the one about the two attorneys who were standing in a field of manure. Suddenly one looked down and said, "My God, we're melting!" For absolutely no reason at all I suddenly remembered that joke, and I thought, lawyers are in no position to discuss bathroom functions.

As the dog vented her opinion of me, the frozen tableau in front of me melted. They moved. Everyone ran to do something.

My housekeeper, Nazalene, went for another clean, dry sweater. Somebody else tore off a paper towel. Since one of us—either the dog or me—was still dribbling, a voice shouted out, "Newspaper. We need newspaper. Somebody find some newspaper."

The nearest one, the one open on the kitchen table, was mine. The *New York Post*. The paper for which I write a gossip column six days a week. It was opened to my page, and the owner of the voice threw it down on the floor.

"NO! Not the *Post*. I don't want this dog doing it on the *Post*, for God's sake. Find something else," I shouted.

"How about the *Times*?" said the voice.

"Yeah. The *New York Times*. Good. Perfect. Turn it to the editorial page," I said, holding the dog straight out and shaking her in an effort to dry off her still dripping whatever.

Too late. This dog took one look at the *New York Post*, and my column definitely caught her interest. She poured all over me.

The two lawyers decided this might be the propitious time to make their good-byes, and they began to put on their hats and coats. "Don't leave empty-handed," I said. "Take your dog with you."

"*Our* dog? He's not our dog," they said.

"What do you mean not your dog. Who brought him? Whose dog is this?"

"We don't know," they said. "He's not our dog. We thought he was your dog."

"*My* dog?" I repeated inanely. "How could it be *my* dog? I don't have a dog."

As my glazed eyeballs began to focus, I saw that one of the humans inside my kitchen was a total stranger.

"Who are you?" I asked.

"Max Courtney, ma'am."

"What's a Max Courtney?"

"Chauffeur, ma'am."

"So? So who are you? What are you doing in my kitchen?"

This nice-looking gray-haired gentleman appeared as tongue-tied as everyone else.

"I'm just doing my job, ma'am."

"Yeah? So? What are you doing in my kitchen? Who did you chauffeur?"

There was a silence, then, "Not who. What."

I was becoming annoyed. "What are you talking about?"

"That." He pointed to the nervous hair ball that was now hanging upside down in my two hands.

As I lowered my hands—the hair ball's docked tail was halfway up my nose—he explained that he worked for a nationwide livery service. His boss at the Manhattan office had received a call from their California base. It was from a customer in Beverly Hills by the name of Michael Viner.

I knew Michael Viner. A TV producer. He and his wife, actress Deborah Raffin, are also copresidents of New Millennium, a house that publishes books on tape. They also happen to be two of my best friends. I'd seen them just a few days earlier. They'd flown to New York for my husband's funeral and back to Los Angeles the next morning.

Yes, I definitely knew Michael Viner. In fact, at that very moment, I was staring at cases and cases of soda stacked up in my pantry. They'd been sent by Michael so I'd have plenty on hand for the well-wishers who'd been dropping by all week to pay their respects.

Seems Michael had decided I needed something in my life. I was newly alone and this aloneness was very fresh. I had no family. No brothers, no sisters, no children. My mother, who was the same age as my husband, no longer

knew who I was. Michael decided I needed something to love. It was a decision, however, that he made unilaterally. Without me.

Michael and Deborah are dog lovers. They've always had dogs. They own two Yorkies, Crillon and Scooter. Scooter they'd recently acquired during a trip east. They'd been driving around Connecticut and passed a sign that said Barnhill Kennels. Within minutes they'd introduced themselves to Paula Segnatelli, breeder of Yorkshire terriers.

This very morning Michael had called Paula and, without asking me anything or telling me anything, inquired if there was any relative of Scooter's available. Paula had one. This one. Scooter's cousin. This one's father and grandfather were champions. This one was a purebred pedigree with the papers and bloodline up the kazoo.

Michael, on the phone from Los Angeles, had told Paula he'd send a limousine to Connecticut to pick up Scooter's baby cousin. The limo had had one sole passenger. In the backseat, all alone. My brand-new, unasked for, unexpected child. His trip in had cost $475.

Six hours later the driver of this limo, who had made contact with my doorman, who had then reached out to my housekeeper, was standing in my kitchen.

It didn't take long—maybe fifteen minutes—and I was already deep in the throes of total panic. This little dog would be looking to me to take care of it, and I had no idea what to do.

I rang Joan Rivers, whose Yorkshire terrier, Spike, was almost a more famous male than John Travolta. But because she's my friend and because it's my job to get gossip items, I asked, "So it shouldn't be a total loss, first tell me how's your love life?"

"Please, the guys I go out with are at the age where they no longer take X rays. The doctor just holds them up to the light. One of them took a nap last week and woke up to discover his water bed broke and he doesn't even have a water bed."

Right. On to the real reason for my call.

"You need Pat McGregor," said Joan, switching instantly from the professional comedian that most people know to the loving human being I know. "Pat McGregor will save your life."

"What's a Pat McGregor?"

"A trainer. The best."

"Okay, what's his number?"

"Not his. Hers."

"What's her number?"

I called Pat McGregor on my other line. Her machine

was on. She was teaching doggy obedience class that night. I wanted desperately to enroll in her owner obedience class. I had no idea what to do.

Animals have a sixth sense. They say a horse knows if a rider's afraid of it. Well, this dog clearly understood that its new adopted parent was a klutz. I hadn't a clue.

"Water. Give her some water." said Joan.

"What kind of water?"

"Look, we're not talking Perrier versus Evian here. Water. Plain water. Water water. She's just made a long trip in by car. She's probably hungry and thirsty. But the first thing is thirsty. Get her some water. Fill a bowl with water and put it down."

I was nervous. I probably could have located the proper bowl if I'd had a moment to collect myself, but I couldn't concentrate. Letters of condolence, sympathy cards, flowers, and messengers and people were arriving steadily. The world was paying its respects to Joey. The doorman kept buzzing and the phones kept ringing. And while I was trying to serve my unexpected live-in and bus the floor in my kitchen, strangers were mixing in my dining room and chatting in my living room.

The kitchen was full of food baskets, trays of cookies, sandwich platters, coffee urns. We couldn't quickly find a bowl that wasn't made out of breakable glass or porcelain.

My hands pounced on some clean plastic container that had earlier contained a half pound of chopped liver. It was a little deep, but at least if it broke this little dog wouldn't cut herself.

I filled it to the top and put it down. I also put the dog down. She ran around. She looked like a little rat.

The dog was jazzed up. Running, darting. She ran right into the water. Foreleg smack into the plastic container. It tipped over. Water was everywhere. She now looked like a drowned rat. I was flat on the floor sopping up this river when the house phone announced that Revlon chairman Ron Perelman and actress Ellen Barkin, his wife, were on their way up.

We quickly piled up some cartons in the kitchen doorway so this doglet couldn't get out and somebody went to fetch some more water and I went forth, smile on my face, pencil in my brain. Because, as Gertrude Stein said, a pro is a pro is a pro. And if Gertrude Stein didn't say it, she would've if she'd thought about it.

In my library sat the Barkin-Perelman pair. Like bookends. Skinny, wearing white shirts and jeans from the same tailor. Speaking of togetherness, they even admitted they had the same-size waistline. The basic difference was Ellen sported a solitaire the size of a pot roast. She also told me she'd just gotten an opera-length string of huge South Sea pearls. "They're my first," Ellen said. I had the feeling that with God's help and Ron's checkbook they wouldn't be her last.

Both were dieting. The perfect guests to have, they barely stayed an hour because neither would eat or drink. As they left I heard a sound I had never heard in my home before.

Barking.

When that evening finally and mercifully drew to an end, I was tired. The last half dozen years watching my husband deteriorate had been exhausting. The last fourteen months had been killing. The last month had been draining. The last week had sucked every drop of blood from my veins.

All I wanted was to turn out the lights and pull the covers over my head. But I couldn't. I didn't know what to do with my new Guest in the House.

Truth is, I didn't even know what to do with myself. I didn't know what to do with my apartment. I'd had so many people sleeping in for so long—maids, nurses, home health-care aides—that I wanted peace. I wanted to be by myself. At this point I wouldn't let even a close friend stay overnight. I wanted, for the moment, to be by myself. I desperately needed to breathe. To think.

For too long I'd been a caregiver. I'd cared for my husband, Joey. I'd cared for my mother, Jessie. I needed not to care about anything or anybody else for now. I didn't need to care if some houseguest needed something to eat or needed another pillow or really needed a cup of Ovaltine when all I had in the house was Sanka. I needed not to care for anybody but myself.

But then, two rooms away, I heard the barking.

I walked in and, with one hand, scooped up this frightened puppy. Her heart was beating so fast. She was trembling. She was just like me. Through some power larger than her own she had been wrenched away from the only family she'd ever known. She was all alone in this big world. She didn't know what was happening to her. She had no idea what the future held. And she was scared.

I understood. I was in the same position. I lay down on my couch and brought her face to face. Nose to nose. Looking her straight in the eyes, I said, "Don't worry, sweetie. We're both in the same boat. We'll take care of one another."

With that she threw up on my chest. It wasn't a whole lot because she wasn't a whole lot. But it was white gook over my throat and nightie. In the instant it took me to stare at the gook and figure out what to grab to wipe it off, the phone rang.

Hillary Clinton.

We knew one another. Years back, while a Marine guard had played the harp outside a private White House dining room, I was teaching her New York street Yiddish. "Schlep" she got right away. "Schmattas" she knew was the word for "rags," junky clothes. She had a little trouble with the word "schloomp." She understood that a schloomp was some sloppy person, but the Illinois/Arkansas/New England background kept mispronouncing it. It kept coming out "schlump." I repeated, "No, Hillary. F'r Crissake, it's the same sound as 'book.'" Sitting in the White House, to the strains of a Marine guard's harp, Mrs. Clinton could be heard reciting "schloomp . . . schloomp . . ."

We'd shared a few stories together over the years, a couple of laughs and one or two tears. It was my original scoop—a whole year before she announced the run for the Senate that she was, indeed, *going* to run for the Senate. Now she was phoning as a friend. Paying her respects. Making the proper bread-and-butter call one makes to another who has just gone through the trauma of a death in the family.

"How are you doing?" she asked.

What am I going to tell her? That this bereaved widow of seven days is crazed? Lying in a pool of gook, struggling to hold onto an itsy, squirming, squiggling, hyped-up, jazzed-up powder puff before her paws ran across me and she tracked the stuff through my house?

We made the usual nobody-quite-knows-what-to-say conversation—*keep your chin up . . . there's life ahead . . . we all have to pay our dues at some point . . . this life is not easy for anyone*—and a few minutes later we hung up.

I decided I had to inform my guest that she really shouldn't repeat what she'd just done. That her behavior really wasn't acceptable or ladylike. I decided to make a bold gesture before explaining the house rules to her. I lifted her high in the air, high over my head with both hands. Only then did I realize she was no lady.

My She was a *He.*

And he would not keep still. Souped up, hyped up, jazzed up. And still trembling. I thought to myself, This must be my karma. It's my duty to be forever a caregiver. Joey . . . Jessie . . . Jazzy . . .

He licked my face.

And I kissed him full on the mouth. "Jazzy, baby, you and me. Together forever."

CHAPTER 3

Call Me Mommy

My husband used to say, "I got into show business so I could sleep late." It was funny then. Not so funny now. All of a sudden wake-up time came at 5 A.M. Me, I could happily have laid around until maybe the crack of seven. It was my new bedmate. Jazzy was like a top sergeant. He got up. Everybody had to get up.

Jazzy had a novel way of sounding reveille. It was silent. No yips, yaps, or woofs. Strictly physical it was. In my deepest sleep I felt the odd sensation of foot nails. This dog woke me by walking across my face. Thank God he was a lapdog. With a Great Dane this could've been a problem.

I knew this was one habit I wanted to break him of, but whom was I going to call at 5 A.M. to start his training?

In fact, who, where, what was I going to do to start anything?

I had my own difficulties to handle before I got rolling on his. Writing a column six days a week, doing lectures, TV commentating, radio interviews, writing magazine pieces—it all takes time. I have a daily routine. And on this day I had my work waiting for me. But now, suddenly, what I also had waiting for me was a brand-new roommate.

"You have to take care of him," said Nazalene. "He's hungry. First thing is, you have to give him food."

"Food. We have loads of food." I opened the fridge and realized instantly that ice-cold, day-old pastrami on stale rye, no matter how much cole slaw and potato salad the Stage Deli had sent over to go with it for the people who were making a shiva call, would not do the job.

"What kind of food?"

"He's a baby. A little baby. He's been away from his mommy for just a day. He needs baby food. For a baby dog. He's only a puppy."

"Yes, okay, I know. I'll get it. But what specifically do I ask for?"

"Dog food. For a baby dog. He's just a *puppy*."

"I understand that. But *what*?"

I called his breeder. Paula told me, "Dry food. Euka-neuba. Little amounts. For right now three times a day. I sent some over with him."

I put her on hold. I looked. I couldn't find it. He didn't exactly come with luggage, and his shopping bag had somehow gotten lost or thrown out.

"So go buy him Eukaneuba."

"Euekawhat?" I couldn't even spell it.

"Eukaneuba. You can give him a tiny tiny tiny little bit of cheese, American cheese. But not much or he'll get the runs. Just a teeny bit. As a treat.

"And everybody thinks you give dogs bones. Wronggg. They crack, and chips can get stuck in his throat. And his water should be bottled water. And make sure you take him to the vet immediately. He has to have shots."

"Vet? What vet? Where do I find a vet?"

"You don't have a vet?" she exclaimed in shock. "What do you mean you don't have a vet? You have to have a vet."

"Why would I have a vet? Until twenty minutes ago I didn't have a dog."

"I'll find you a vet. And don't forget you have to cut the hair around his ears so that the weight of it doesn't pull down his ears. They must stand up, because he's a champion. You should actually register him with the Westminster Kennel. They'll cut a slight V-shape away from the hair so that the ear doesn't fold over."

"Who's *they*?"

"The groomer."

"This thing is six inches long and he already has a trainer and a breeder and a groomer?"

"Don't forget the vet."

Michael Viner called.

"I can't talk to you," I said. "I have to run out quickly and get your present some Eukaneuba."

"Why Eukaneuba?"

"Because that's what the breeder said."

"Oh, please. We feed ours chicken, no skin, cut up small, and mashed with a little rice."

"Paula said Eukaneuba."

"What do you have at home? Chicken?"

"Pastrami."

"Okay, so get the Eukaneuba. But they like a tiny bit of wet food so mix it with wet food."

"*What* wet food? What are you talking about? This isn't Le Cirque. This animal that I've fallen heir to is a few minutes old and I'm already a cordon bleu chef. Look, I don't know what I'm supposed to do."

"Fine," said Michael. "What you're supposed to do is give him chicken. Without the skin."

I realized quickly the difference between coochie-cooing this baby and actually tending to its needs. It was delicious to pet Jazzy, but I wasn't prepared to *care* for him.

He had *needs*. He had to eat, be made strong and healthy and safe, get a license, get an ID, get friends, get a spot to sleep. I didn't know what to do first.

But he did.

He pooped smack on my right foot.

My friend Tommy called. Tommy has had dogs forever. He said, "You need to buy puppy papers."

"What do puppy papers do?"

"They're for pooping."

"What's he need a paper to poop on! He's already found my right foot."

I made a list. Day one of things to buy for Jazzy's requirements.

As I was leaving, the phone rang. The Buckingham Palace press officer, treating me like the commoner he knew me to be. I'd reported a scoop in my column that Prince Charles had done a U.S. TV interview. I even knew when it was to air. The press officer was in a huff. About my Prince Charles interview exclusive, he sniffed, "Impossible, madam."

I told him I was unaware that the queen had a sub-scription to the *New York Post*. I said that, between ruling her country and her family, I couldn't imagine she'd man-aged to read my column. I related to him the precise date this interview in question had been taped, that it was late afternoon on Smith's Lawn, Windsor Great Park. That HRH sported a double-breasted blue blazer with gold buttons and four matching sleeve buttons, red bouton-niere, blue-and-red striped tie, blue foulard hanky, striped shirt, gold pinky ring, pin-on mike, and that I'd seen the bloody film with my own eyes.

What I didn't tell him was that, at that precise instant in time, I couldn't have cared less. The only royal that could remotely have attracted my attention this particular day was a King Charles spaniel.

I had my list. On it was Eukaneuba, chicken, Ameri-can cheese, puppy papers. Also his own bowls. One for water, one for food. Then, since he was teething, chew toys. Like rubber duckies and Naugahyde bones. And treats. He needed treats. And a leash, a collar, a bed, heartworm pills. A coat, a sweater, a blanket. Also a carry-ing bag. And not to forget Febreze to neutralize the aroma if he did something in the wrong place.

❧

In the twinkling of an eyelash, Jazzy took over my heart. Little by little he was taking over my life. He began within a week by taking over my apartment. For the second time in recent history, my home had to be turned upside down to accommodate a male. The first order of business was to devise a way to protect my artifacts from Jazzy's incisors.

Since there was no portion of chow, Pekingese, shih tzu, or any breed that had any Eastern background in Jazzy, I could not understand his obsession with Asian treasures. However, he was like an art dealer I'd known once in England. This dealer could smell a copy from an original at one hundred paces. Jazzy's nose was still better. He wouldn't even go in the same room with a fakola.

He was partial to Ming. Chewing the leg of a table that once belonged to a fourteenth-century Mandarin gave him lots more pleasure than gnawing away at a stick that once belonged to some forty-year-old maple.

Jazzy, a confirmed New Yorker, was into eating Chinese.

I tried telling him he couldn't do that. Stuff like, "No, no, no, no . . . bad dog . . . Mommy doesn't like that."

Please. He just cocked his head to one side and looked at me as though to say, "Listen, I know your type. My mother was also a bitch."

Canine behaviorists suggest a spray, Bitter Apple, which generates a sour taste so that your pet won't want to go there again. I bought several bottles. Unfortunately, one of its components is alcohol, which wears off after it hits the air. You thus must respray. I became weary of bending over like a hoop or getting down on my hands and knees to again and again and again respray. All this only to have my dog, who was considerably smarter than I, and was just standing off to one side waiting until I stopped making a jerk of myself, come back and chew away at his favorite Ming leg.

The solution was to declare certain areas off-limits. Not give him the run of the house. Contain him. Make his permanent home the kitchen. This is not exactly a hardship. We are not talking some dim dungeon here. Since we'd redone the kitchen to accommodate Joey, it had remained the large, bright family room in which the whole household lives.

To confine the dog I needed gates. I went shopping for baby gates. One style I found was too low. It seems infants don't pole-vault. Another allowed too much space between it and the doorjambs to which it would be attached. A chunky, chubby toddler wouldn't wriggle through. Jazzy would.

I finally found attractive but heavy-duty plastic doggy

gates that were adjustable to the width of any door. They worked fine; the lone difficulty was that they had no latch to open and close them so they could swing out like a garden gate when you wanted to pass through.

My kitchen has two entrances. Thus, two doggy gates were needed to contain this new man of the house and prevent him from making our entire home a garbage can. Physically having to remove each gate the thousand times any of us had to go through it in a day was absolutely not feasible. So the result was, no matter who, no matter how famous, no matter how arthritic, no matter even if you were a VIP female guest of a certain age, you hoisted your legs over and across those stupid doggy gates.

It caused some embarrassment. It also caused a lot of expense.

I was a dog owner—mommy barely a week, and my new child had already cost me more than my husband did all year.

CHAPTER 4

Our First Christmas

O nly three weeks had passed since Joey had gone, and it was holiday season. My head wasn't into caroling. The house was empty. No tree, no decorations. No joy. Just Jazzy and me and the Ghost of Christmas Past.

This very first Christmas without Joey I was feeling sorry for myself. I found myself thinking about the story Joey had told me long ago about his very first Christmas. He was then alone. I was now alone. Suddenly I could relate.

We're going back a lifetime ago. Somewhere around our fifteenth anniversary, one quiet night when the rain was falling softly and this dynamo I had married was feeling mellow, he told me about his very first Christmas. I wasn't there at the time. I wasn't even born at the time.

It harked back to his first professional job. He was maybe seventeen, trying out in vaudeville, working the State Theater in Baltimore. A kid who was heavy on energy and ambition, what he was light on was experience and talent. A brash front tried to mask the inadequacies.

It was Christmas Eve. Joey didn't know from Christmas. His mother and father were Orthodox Jews. But that night, standing outside the stage door, all alone in a strange city with no friends or family, he could see lights blinking on and off. He was staring at a Christmas tree.

The young, lonely boy dug his hand in his pocket. His palm revealed that he was worth $1.85. "I can do it for that," he thought.

He jumped into his coat and wool stocking cap and ran to the supermarket near the theater. For a dollar he bought almost more potato chips, peanuts, pretzels, and popcorn than he could carry. Ten cents went for paper plates. He hauled his stash back to the theater. Laying all the food out on the dozen paper plates, he set them on whatever chairs and upended crates he found backstage and stepped back to survey his display. "Maybe it's not great," he thought, "but at least it's beginning to look like Christmas. Now, if only I had a tree."

The future big-time comedian was still worth another seventy-five cents. His worldly goods. All he had left in the world. He ran back out to the street, hunting a tree. Two blocks down he found a street corner seller who had the remnants of a Christmas sale. There were only a few wreaths and sickly branches left. Joey blew his whole capital on, as he put it to me many years later, "a skinny, bare hunk of scraggly foliage that was naked six inches from the top."

In Joey's words, "By the time I dragged the tree back, I felt a little ashamed. The thing looked even more anemic now than it had on the street corner. And I had no money left for decorations.

"Back into the deserted theater again, I rummaged through the big garbage can and came up with empty cigarette packages, a few used ribbons from Christmas parcels that had been opened backstage, and some gold foil from holiday cigars.

"I meticulously stripped the tinfoil from the cigarette packages and tied the strips to the branches. I did the same with the gold foil. Then I spliced the ribbon and draped it around other branches. I took the gold-tone pen and pencil set my mom had given me for graduation and hung them on the tree, too.

"Then I stood back to view my handiwork. While it had given the withered pine some small semblance of life, it definitely was not what got lit up at Rockefeller Center."

Joey had invited everyone on the bill. The acrobat, the dance team, the juggler, the over-the-hill female singer. But he hadn't made any friends. He acknowledged to me that he was about as popular "as a stripper at a DAR convention." His act wasn't ready. He wasn't ready. And so he had overcompensated by blaming everyone. Scared, nervous, all bluff, he put down the audience when his jokes fell flat. "You must eat your young in this town." Ba-dum-bum.

Joey, who was barely old enough to shave, picked a fight with the veteran stagehand because the curtain came down before his big laugh started up. Of course, the reason that the curtain came down before Joey's big laugh started up was simple. The stagehand knew if he'd waited for the big laugh, they'd still be there.

By 10:30 nobody had shown up for Joey's party. "They must have stopped off for a drink someplace," he told himself. "They'll be here any minute." That minute stretched to 11:30, and still none of the invited guests had arrived.

He looked at the tree, and as he recalled it to me many

years later, "In my bitterness, the Yuletide glow was gone. Sitting in my lonely little dressing room, I saw it for what it really was. The tree was a consumptive-looking scruffy growth with rubbish hanging from it. The sight of it made me sick."

Fade-in/fade-out. That lonely night was a long time ago and the last time he was ever alone on Christmas. What I was living through now, at this very moment, was a very different Christmas. But I was also alone. That early Joey memory was almost gone. Joey, too, was gone. All that was left was what was left of me.

I missed him. I had several invitations for this holiday that was suddenly upon me, but I'd made no plans. There is a saying that a new leaf cannot form on a tree until the old leaf falls. I was in an emotional hallway. Making my way through that dark, narrow path that had seen one light flicker out and, now, another trying to shine in. It was a transition period. I was moving out artifacts, possessions, and mementos of a love I had shared, and I was moving in the appurtenances, necessaries, and where-withal of a love I was about to know.

Christmas Eve I heard from Imelda Marcos. She announced that she was in town and planned to spend

Christmas Day with me. I've known the former first lady of the Philippines since we were both invited to the Shah of Iran's two thousandth anniversary of the Persian empire in 1971. His Majesty had built a tent city upcountry in Persepolis, and wall-to-wall VIPs such as Imelda, Princess Grace of Monaco, Emperor Haile Selassie of Ethiopia, and then–Vice President Spiro Agnew were guests. Imelda and I struck up a friendship. In the mid-seventies I arranged for the Miss Universe Pageant to televise from Manila.

Imelda and I had spent months together organizing that project. Just for the one-shot telecast she had built a multimillion-dollar theater. It was subsequently to be the centerpiece of an art compound, but its birth was to house the pageant that was beaming live from Manila to five hundred million viewers worldwide. The program was to be a great tourist attraction for the Philippines as well as a great frame for the first lady of the country, Mrs. Ferdinand Marcos.

The plan was to televise 9 A.M. Sunday morning, which would be 9 P.M. Saturday night in New York— New York being the hub. All was arranged.

The theater had been designed to be open on three sides. Exactly two days before the show there were hurricane warnings. The information coming in was that this could be a killer storm. The pageant did not have hurricane insurance. Hurried, panicked telephone calls to brokers around the world did not produce the necessary coverage. Conference calls to sponsors went on all night long. Our hotline to CBS in New York was working on a cancellation rain date.

Imelda summoned us to Malacanan Palace. "Don't worry," she said. "I will not allow a hurricane."

"Not allow" a hurricane? Come again, lady?

With the Oriental calm I would see her display years later when she was on trial and facing prison, she said, "I will not allow a hurricane. I will send the Philippine Air Force up to seed the clouds."

And that's what she did. Sent Filipino pilots up in fragile Piper Cubs to deposit the silver nitrate or whatever it is that weights those black, angry clouds so that they float out to sea. And float out they did. They cleared the dark skies around the main island of Luzon in a fifty-mile radius.

The sun shone that Sunday morning in all its brilliant glory. The pageant went on. Two days later the clouds floated back in, the heavens opened, and the city was under a sea of water. The main street, Roxas Boulevard, was waist deep in water. We were all locked in. Nobody could get out of Manila for two days. But Imelda had saved the pageant.

Over the years we've seen one another in varying parts of the world. When Mrs. Marcos was exiled from her country and indicted in ours, I reported on her story daily. I was in Hawaii when her husband, the president, died. She was in New York for Joey's funeral.

So, like an old friend, Imelda said she wanted to come over Christmas Day. To commiserate a little. Sit and talk. Have a bite.

Imelda arrived at ten-thirty Christmas morning. I was alone in the apartment. Just me and my dog. Everyone was off. I was still in the Egyptian galabaya—a white, floor-length Arab men's shirt I always wear around the house. In good light you can see through the thing. It's cotton. I hadn't even added a slip. We were just two ladies who had known one another thirty years. My hair was in a tangle. Uncombed. Straight from bed. And I hadn't any makeup on. In fact, there was still some chicken fat or whatever that I'd slathered on my face the night before.

In comes Imelda like something out of *Women's Wear.* Red designer suit. Clunky, chunky gold jewelry. Remember her collection of shoes? Well, these were red suede Manolo Blahniks. And she was made up as if for a Sharon Stone close-up. Me, I looked like five miles of bad road.

We spoke for hours, sharing memories of better days. Imelda laughingly recalled the time I'd flown across the world to see her and she gave me a dinner party as I stepped off the plane. She'd seated me next to President Marcos and, due to jet lag, I fell asleep during the soup and my head flopped right on his shoulder.

She spoke of Doris Duke, who'd been her neighbor during the Marcoses' years of exile in Makiki Heights, Honolulu. Doris had come up with the five million dollars' bail money needed to keep Imelda out of jail. The apartment I now lived in was a familiar one to Imelda. It had been Doris Duke's for thirty years. I had bought it from her estate, and Imelda was eager to see the changes. After we'd run through the girl talk, she took a tour. And then we were hungry. We decided to dispatch her security for Big Macs, fries, and coffee.

My kitchen has a service door. Imelda's bodyguard was standing right outside this door, which opens to a little hallway and our elevator. As the hours ticked by, Imelda, in pencil-slim skirt and stiletto heels, had repeatedly lumbered back and forth over our doggy gates. At this moment, when hunger had overtaken us, those nice first lady legs had grown tired. There seemed no reason once more to hitch up her skirt and tour j'eté over that damn doggy gate just to come back into the kitchen and open that service door to speak to the bodyguard.

So we opened the front door. Jazzy heard the sound. Jazzy began barking frantically inside the kitchen, crazed that we might be leaving him alone. Distracted, I neglected to turn the safety bolt, and the front door slammed shut behind us.

There we were. In this small vestibule facing the elevator. No key. The superintendent was away. It was Christmas. The building staff does not have access. Nazalene was off. My phone was ringing. My dog was inside barking. And we were staring at one another in panic.

She couldn't take me to her hotel because I could scarcely trot through the lobby in my see-through, egg-stained rag. Besides, her purse was sitting on my kitchen table.

The bodyguard eventually returned with two greasy brown paper bags. And until a locksmith arrived, there we sat, the former first lady of the Republic of the Philippines, in designer suit, designer shoes, designer jewelry, designer makeup, and me with my behind hanging out, eating Christmas dinner with our fingers. Big Macs and fries, on paper napkins on our laps on the floor.

And it was all Jazzy's fault.

CHAPTER 5

Bed Luck

Stress is a killer, and it had been a stressful year. I was not feeling well. My mind and body were at war with me. Sleep had become a stranger. No matter how I hugged the pillows, they refused to be friendly. I couldn't find a resting place in my own bed.

In the middle of the night, when the surrounding world was black, the devil paid his visits. We're talking hobgoblin time. Thoughts spun round and round in my head, refusing to be quieted. Memories of the end, the day Joey died. Replays of the indignities. Questions about what would happen to me. As the images poured into my

weary brain, I sought to make some sense of it all—what my life with Joey had meant and what it was I was missing now.

A few weeks before Joey left us, Barbara Walters and I shared a quiet dinner together. Barbara and I have known one another a lifetime. Back when she was a schoolgirl headed for stardom and I was a schoolgirl headed for wifehood, we met in the Latin Quarter nightclub. Her father, Lew Walters, owned it. My fiancé, Joey Adams, starred in it. A load of exclusive stories later we're still friends. We have apartments a few blocks from one another. On this evening we shared memories, good and bad. Barbara had seen me at Joey's side supplying the name of a longtime friend he could no longer recall. She'd watched me buttering his cracker in a restaurant. She knew. And Barbara could ask the question many had only pondered silently. Drawing on the right of friendship, she said to me, "Certainly you could have done something else with your personal life. So, why? Why did you stay? Why did you stick it out all these years?"

"You never leave a party except with the fellow who brought you," was my answer. This man gave me everything. Everything I have I got from him. He introduced me to the world. My meeting those people, experiencing those experiences, seeing their oddities, was the begin-

ning of what I do and what I am today. Maybe I stuck it out because he never made me cry. Never hurt me. Never let me down. Maybe I stayed because life with Joey was like covering yourself with a pair of Dr. Denton's. Warm, fuzzy, comfortable. Maybe it's that I knew if I ever got fat or ugly or if, in the blinding sunshine of a beach day, my facial fuzz would show, he'd still be there.

But now he wasn't there, and the shadows kept me up at night. All I could do was grab naps on the couch in my office.

Unfortunately, the width of a sofa doesn't allow enough room for two bodies, even when one's only the length of a king-size hot dog.

It was a stormy, rainy night when I squashed my new roommate. My huge 120-pound frame suddenly gave itself a change of position. Jazzy had somehow located that little hollow in the small of my back and balled himself up there, and I rolled right over onto him. My hips pinioned him against the back of the couch. He gave an anguished squeal and hobbled off me and off the couch. Trust me, if a Yorkie could give you the finger, this beauty would've.

That's when I made a right turn mentally and took a shot at returning to the bedroom. But I was going to be doing it without my dog, who presently wanted no part of

me. I came to the realization that I was going to have to entice him into my bed. It was as though you'd had a fight with your lover and had to lure him back under the sheets. This fella did not want to go. His look said, "Screw you," and off he padded in another direction. Not that I look like Pamela Anderson or anything, but I haven't really had to play heavy games to get a male creature into my bed since I had my nose done at age sixteen.

The bed was cold. It was empty. Unwelcoming. And this little boy whom I had mashed was not interested. He was not happy with me. I waved a snippet of American cheese, for which he'd normally kill. Nothing. I placed a Milk-Bone on the sheet. No dice. I pulled out my bag of tricks. How could I go to sleep without Jazzy curved around me? I put his favorite food out and stuck it near me. The bowl tipped over and my mattress ended up smelling of Alpo, but Jazzy wouldn't bite.

Diane Von Furstenburg wrote a book on beds a few years ago. The beautiful beds of the beautiful people. I don't do particularly well with beds. I don't mean what I do *in* them. I mean beds and I somehow don't make it.

My string of bad luck bedwise had begun back in Bangkok. Joey was doing a charity performance for Their

Majesties King Bhumibol and Queen Sirikit of Thailand. I have known the queen for decades. I was even involved in helping to bring her handicrafts to the United States. Maybe thirty years ago we first sat for hours in the gardens of her all-white Chitralada Palace deep in the heart of Bangkok. It was its usual 100 degrees in the shade. And there was no shade. I was perspiring. Patting myself and fanning myself and reapplying powder with the zeal of an engineer filling in a sinking beach. Not once in those four hours did Sirikit reach for her handkerchief, a piece of Kleenex, nothing. I couldn't stand it. I said to her, "Your Majesty, you may be a queen but, after all, you are a human being. Don't you ever have to fan yourself or pat yourself?" She said, "I have made up my mind I won't perspire—and I don't."

So we were again in Thailand. We had a suite. We were there five nights. Each night we were there and for no reason I could figure, the sofa bed in the living room was opened, extended lengthwise across the room, and made up for sleeping. After the first night I explained to our chambermaid, "See, we are only two people. And we are married. We don't need a sofa bed opened in the living room."

The chief housekeeper apologized. She said, "The previous occupants were in residence a while and they had children. Therefore the night room attendant has become accustomed to making up the living room sofa bed for sleeping. I will explain to her. It won't happen again."

The second night it happened again. I explained again. Also the third night. That sofa bed was still always opened, extended across the whole room, and made up for sleeping. In the wee hours of the fourth night, our living room phone rang. I ran to answer it. In the blackness I fell across the opened sofa bed, gashed my leg on the corner of the iron frame, and ended up on the floor cut deeply and bleeding badly.

My string of bad luck bedwise continued on to Kuala Lumpur. Malaysia is hot and steamy. The hotel had the air-conditioning up so high I was shivering. I called down to have someone come up and repair the thing, but it was 2 A.M. and this wasn't about to happen in a big hurry since they had to go roust out some technician. Besides, in that part of the world the efficiency is not exactly Teutonic. My fingers were freezing. I could not figure how to shut the thing off or turn it down. I thus did the only intelligent thing a person could do, the only option left open to me. I cursed the stupid thermostat, then hammered it repeatedly with a shoe. Nothing. I wrapped myself in my floor-length mink coat (it had been winter in New York when I left) and threw myself into bed. How would I know that, because I was doing an interview with the king, security guards would be posted outside my door? Their information was that I was all alone behind that door. So when they heard angry shouting and loud banging, they burst in. To find what? A terrified female in bed in their tropical country wearing an ankle-length mink with a fur hood covering her face.

On another occasion, the location was Tahiti. Marlon Brando's hideaway. In the front yard were young green coconuts, lush South Pacific foliage, vermilion and purple and orange flowers, banana trees, papaya trees, mango trees, and a souped-up motorcycle. Or at least that's how it was when Joey and I were there.

Tarita Teriipaia, mother of Marlon's youngest son, Teihotu, and his only daughter, Cheyenne, invited us in. She had no help in the four-bedroom house. "I do everything," she said in a pussy willow voice. "All the cooking and washing and cleaning. When Marlon is here he wants to relax, so it isn't right to have anyone in to disturb him. Sometimes he helps a little around the house, although not too much."

She pointed to the living room floor. "I personally put down all that straw matting. And I myself sewed those long yellow drapes and white curtains. I am the one who hung them on the windows, too."

It was our first visit to Tahiti, which, even without visiting Brando's home, was an extravagant experience. The island is a paradise. To extend hospitality the hotel had put us in a private bungalow, fashioned in the style of a thatched hut. Lovely. Beautiful. Unfortunately, Joey was never outdoorsy. He might even have made do with a closet as long as it was in the main building close to an elevator. No, they said, we wouldn't think of it. This is for VIPs. This is the utmost in privacy. Me, I'd been married since the year of the Flood. Boy, did I not need privacy. Anyway, that's where they put us.

It rained. At night when the rain stopped I heard little rubbing sounds in the thatch directly above where we were sleeping. Somebody said it was probably termites in the wood beams, but we shouldn't worry. They wouldn't hurt us. Just to be on the safe side we made them move the bed. Next day it rained again. Next night the rubbing sounds again. We made them move the bed again. Third night the bed collapsed under us.

My bed luck had followed me across the world. With deep apologies to the memory of my late husband, I hardly ever enjoyed great evenings in bed.

And now again, in my new life, another kerfuffle. I was leaving the couch behind forever and going into our bedroom. Ultimately, Jazzy decided he'd give me another chance. Maybe it was the alternatives. His bed and my throw rug were comfy but lonely. Back he came to snuggle himself right up against me. He made no apologies. He showed no embarrassment. He simply reclaimed what he considered his rightful place. Just like a male, I thought. With the sweet happiness afforded me by having this delicious being curled right around me came problems again.

It was aches and pains once more. I felt I was becoming arthritic. One of Jazzy's favored spots was my chest. I felt I had to put my hand around him so that if I shifted positions he wouldn't tumble off. But to shift positions would disturb him. Therefore, most times, I tried not to move. After an extended period, however, my fingers would freeze and my elbow would desperately need to be flexed.

If I turned on my side, in the spoon position, he'd burrow up against the back of my knees. To unlock those knees as the hours ticked away and to straighten those legs would be to remove that little hollow which had become his bunk. The result? I'd lie there far into the night with numbed calves.

This being a new room and new sleeping arrangements, we both had to adjust to unfamiliar atmospheric conditions. I liked to keep the window open at night, and it was a bit chilly in the room for my little ball of fluff. He crept under the quilt. And remained there. The whole night. No movement. No air. I stayed rigid out of fear he'd become asphyxiated and I wouldn't know. I was up the entire time. Periodically, as the whole eastern seaboard other than myself lay in dreamland, I was awake sticking my hand under the duvet to make sure he was breathing. Forget about wanting to get up in the middle of the night to go to the john or get a drink of water or lean over to scribble a note about something that just flashed through my mind. I couldn't bear to disturb that tiny hank of hair that was burrowed into my bones.

I wasn't getting any sleep. I was exhausted. Part of the job requirement of a columnist who writes about celebrities is to spot them, schmooze them and, you hope, extract a worthwhile printable newsy comment from them. However, I was plain groggy from lack of rest. So weary that the maître d' in one restaurant had to whisper to me, "Look who you walked right by."

I looked. Twiggy! I know and like Twiggy and wouldn't slight her for the world. So I walked back. "Hi, Twig," I twittered and sat down uninvited. "I apologize for not recognizing you, but I'm a little off tonight."

She made a few minutes of sweet conversation, but suddenly I stood up. "Twiggy, you know I love you and I'd like to stay and gab, but you'll just have to excuse me for dashing off. I've got to get home and get some sleep. I'll explain another time."

I gave her a quick hug with, "'Bye, Twig." I sensed she was eyeing me oddly, but I scooted off.

The next morning the restaurant owner called to ask if I was all right. "Why?" I asked.

"Because you were talking to Goldie Hawn."

Only God in his infinite wisdom can divine what a death this was for a gossip columnist.

The neck and back became my major disability. A searing pain pierced my neck every time I turned my head right or left. And if I had to bend, to put on a shoe or stocking, I almost couldn't bear the agonizing stabs. In trying to find a comfortable place for myself in my own bed while accommodating my dog, I had switched to sleeping flat on my back. The new pillows were stiff. While my body was flat, my neck had remained propped up. It was causing me great distress. At the hairdresser, while I was seated in the shampoo section, they lowered my head to the sink and I literally could not bear it.

My hairdresser, Lisa, asked me in a suggestive tone, "What's with the pains in your body? You had a great time last night?"

Go tell her my partner in bed was the size of an earmuff. She'd think I was mentally disturbed.

The neck pains were such that I could no longer lie flat, so I went back to my side. My dog, way under the quilt, with his head in his favorite hanging-down position, curved around my hip. His tail was pointed toward my face, his ears to my knee. If I moved, it was slight and with great deliberation. I most often remained bent into an unnatural shape.

My body lay twisted night after night like a pretzel. Not until daylight would I shift myself. No wonder I was aching and paining.

I fretted this was arthritis. Then bursitis. Then neuritis. Then rheumatoiditis. And then I realized—it's Jazzyitis. Psychologists say I'll have difficulty with my dog if ever I want to put a man in my bed. Listen, who has room for a man in my bed? There's not even room for *me* in my bed.

CHAPTER 6

It's a Dog's Life

A brand-new puppy in your house is like a brand-new marriage to a sex addict. Crazy and exciting—for about two weeks. Then, much as you love it, come the headaches.

I guess I'm not alone in having such headaches. Going crosstown one early morning, I saw a little old lady yanking on the leash of her dachshund, who was being uncooperative. Finally she shouted at him, "How many times do I have to tell you that? Don't you understand English?"

I knew my hound was destined to grow. A Great Dane he'd never be, but for sure he had to blossom beyond the eight inches at which he seemed to be plateauing. I was hoping for more *presence* because I was tripping over him on a regular basis. It's not as if I'd always had a live silver-and-rust pouf beneath my spike heels. I wasn't accustomed to looking out and under. This was all new to me.

There was the time I turned my ankle because I had to pivot about sharply to avoid stepping on him. There was the time he nearly got sucked into the vacuum because nobody knew he was there. There was the time a delivery man set the groceries down on top of him. And there was the time Tova Borgnine tripped over him.

Let it be known that Ernest Borgnine and his wife, who created the Tova cosmetics empire, are not queasy around animals. Oh God, are they not queasy. I learned that fast when the Borgnines arranged a little lunch for me in Tova's pink office in Los Angeles. The place card to my right said, "Sasha." No last name.

Suddenly there was a large commotion downstairs. People scuffling. Chains rattling. Sasha had arrived.

We're talking a sleek brunette. Like eight feet worth. *Long*, not tall. With yellow eyes and whiskers only an electrolysist would love to touch. Sasha was a full-size, full-grown, full-blood, full-fur black panther. My luncheon partner summed up our amazement quickly. "Holy shit," were his exact words.

I found my voice first. "*This* is sitting next to me?

What's she going to want me to pass—the person across the table?"

Sasha, whose form graced the logo of Tova's skin care corporation, starred in all her ads. Tova had thought meeting her would make a great column for me. This major predator who stalks the jungle had to travel with her handlers in a transport cage loaded onto a truck, and the entire cage came up in the freight elevator. To bring her to lunch, Tova was made to buy a multimillion-dollar liability policy with an additional million-dollar rider from the City Council of Beverly Hills.

The handlers kept Sasha on a very tight leash, which was extremely okay by me. The leash was a thick, thick chain—the kind that attaches to the anchor of a battleship. One of our tablemates whispered, "They couldn't have a spaniel for a logo?"

This was a fairly laid-back cat. Bared her fangs only six times. The handlers kept both hands wrapped around the chain, very close to Sasha's neck. In a low voice the lady handler said, "Do not try to pet her."

I mean, was she nuts?

"Sit, stand, or move slowly," ordered the handler. "Walk, do not run, or she'll think you're prey. Keep quiet. Don't yell or scream."

"How about telling *her* how to behave," I mumbled.

"Don't do anything to scare her."

"*We're* scaring *her*?"

"Sasha has an agent," said Tova.

"She gone up for any movie parts lately?" I asked.

Looking at me quietly, the lead handler replied, "Sasha does not audition. She's already got the part."

Yeah, right.

"We cannot be sure how long she'll stay because if she suddenly decides she doesn't like somebody we have to take her out of here."

"How can you tell when she doesn't like you?" I asked.

The handler blinked at me and answered softly, "She'll let you know."

Yeah, right.

I don't know exactly how long Sasha stayed, but I got the hell out of there fast.

So, like I said, Tova knows from animals. But mine she had a problem with. She couldn't get out of his way because she couldn't keep track of where he was and so she tumbled over him. Little dogs can be a problem, and I was such a new parent that I was no help in solving anything. About all I could contribute to any situation was fear. I was mostly paralyzed with fright at all the things that could go wrong. And did.

❧

In spite of my fears, I was eager to introduce Jazzy to the world. And so, on an unseasonably warm winter Saturday, I decided to take Jazzy on an outing. I planned to introduce him to birds, squirrels, grass—the works. This city boy of mine was going to take a day's drive into the world outside Manhattan.

I don't remember where exactly I meandered, but it was off the main road. I left the highway and turned onto a one-lane byway where nothing existed for miles but marsh and flatland and nature. The lone structure to interrupt this pastoral peace was a small shed. A rickety wooden table with a hand-lettered sign reading, "Homemade preserves."

I stopped to pick up a couple jars of strawberry jam and got right back into the car. I had gas in the tank, Harry Connick, Jr., on the radio, money in my pocket, my dog with me, and if anyone swore heaven was better than this I wouldn't have believed it.

A little while down the road I felt around behind me for Jazzy, who'd left my lap to try out the fur blanket on the backseat.

I couldn't find him. I slowed down and scrooched

myself around so that my left hand could wriggle way along the inside of my driver's seat door and into the back.

I couldn't touch him.

"Jazzy," I called. "Jazzy-poo."

Nothing. No answer.

I shouted, "Jazzy . . . Jazzy . . . JAZZZZEEEEEE . . . !!!"

No Jazzy. My dog wasn't there. *There was no dog!*

I pulled over to the side of the road and investigated my car. No Jazzy. My heart in my mouth, I made the fastest U-turn in captivity and raced back to the shed.

The nice old farmer said he hadn't seen my dog.

I didn't know what to do. Obviously something must have happened, but what? I didn't know what. I didn't even know where to start because there was no place to go. It was total isolation. Nothing around. There was no place to search. No homes, no stores, no signs of life.

I was distraught. I begged the man, "Please, I have a dog but he's not here. Please help me."

"We-ell, maybe yer little feller's with mine."

"What little feller you talking about?"

Seems the farmer had a dog. An outdoor mutt who was born locally and knew the terrain and had become very used to scampering off and then wandering back when he was ready.

"You just best wait," he said.

"Wait? Like how long?"

"Like 'til he comes, I guess."

I was hysterical. I kept babbling, "You think anything possibly could have happened to my dog?"

"Naaah. He's safe. Nobody'll do nothin' to him here. Only problem in these parts is snakes."

Snakes!

"Please. Advise me. Tell me what to do."

"Wait."

I waited. I could hardly leave. I just hung around and waited. I sat there. I walked up and down. I went back to the car. I walked some more. I was desperate. I was obsessing. "My dog couldn't just have disappeared. I mean, he wouldn't just pick up and leave."

"Your dog must have likely run off with my dog."

Calmly going about his business, the farmer paid my crisis no mind since he clearly never paid a lot of attention to his outdoor mutt, who was familiar with the neighboring countryside.

"Oh, my God, I don't know what to do," I repeated inanely.

"Wait."

I waited. Five hours I waited. Then, way in the distance, waaaayyyy off in the distance, I espied two specks. The specks grew larger as they headed our way. My heart

skipped a beat. Over the horizon trotted a weary Jazzy Adams and his new best friend, Farmer Mutt.

Except for the fact that I probably lost a few pounds from having sweated for hours, this was not an experience I ever wanted to repeat. The lone bit of good to come out of it was that I eventually came up with the idea of hanging a teeny bell on Jazzy's collar. This way we could hear him whenever and wherever he wobbled, even if it was just around the house.

It worked. It solved the problem. But the weather turned cold, and the heat in my apartment blasted away. It was too warm inside to keep a collar around Jazzy's neck. No problem. Where was he going to go?

That morning we took off the collar. It was a really busy Monday. None of us had even noticed Jazzy sneaking out the service door. And thank the Lord our people in the building found him. When I realized what had happened, I panicked. He was so little anyone could've scooped him up. He even could've wobbled into one of the garbage sacks. Without a collar, he had no ID on him. Who knew when and where we'd find him?

There's only one other apartment on my floor. My neighbors are a charming, elegant couple. He was Clinton's ambassador to Denmark. They have very high-level evenings. Definitely not piano-playing beer and karaoke

events. More like black-tie galas for Her Majesty the queen of Denmark.

That evening, Ambassador Ed Elson and his wife, Susie, were having the royalty over for a sit-down. Our little mutual vestibule was filled with coat racks, catering equipment, champagne bottles, flower deliveries, and all sorts of strangers coming and going and delivering.

Mid-gala, whilst servants in white coats and gloves darted yon and thither, whilst glorious ladies in even more glorious satin ball gowns and diamond tiaras were curtsying, our bell rang.

Seems, despite guys wandering around with dark glasses, buttons on their lapels, phones in their ears, and transmitters on their wrists, the security had been broken. This super-high-level soiree had experienced a crasher.

I opened the door, and there stood Ambassador and Mrs. Elson's housekeeper. Smiling broadly. And holding Jazzy in her arms. She'd discovered him standing alongside her waiting politely for her to precede him into the service elevator.

Despite the breach of protocol, I was proud of him. I mean, at least he was a gentleman.

CHAPTER 7

Trainer Hell

After only four months, Jazzy, the resident top dog, was running our whole house. He needed a trainer. Me, I also needed a trainer. Actually, everyone I knew had a personal trainer. I felt so ashamed that I was almost the only one I knew who was trainerless.

I wondered, where did I go wrong? Was it something my best friends wouldn't tell me? Had I failed the bad breath test?

Forgetting the dog for a moment, the biggest problem for me was that I didn't seem to know why I, my very own human self, would need a personal trainer. Okay, so my behind had infinitesimally enlarged to the size of a hammock. Okay, so I for a fact did not fit into last year's sheaths. But my own personal trainer?

When my grandma sailed from the old country and took up residence on the Lower East Side and made home-cooked chicken soup that was the consistency of melted Vaseline and so thick it would bend the spoon, she had a personal trainer?

I knew I was missing out, but I didn't know what to do about it when my high-class friends, definitely much higher class than I am myself, would tell me, "Sorry, can't meet you for late lunch Thursday because that's the time my personal trainer comes over."

Oh, sorry, excuse me. I would never interfere with your personal trainer. The truth is, I didn't 100 percent know what a personal trainer did.

One day, visiting a society friend, I asked, "Why do you need ten rooms? You live alone." She explained that each room was accounted for, including, "And one is a gym."

Right. In a Fifth Avenue apartment, everyone needs a gym. She explained there was no place else to stick her personal trainer.

Right. How stupid of me not to have considered that.

In the old days a high-class person had a secretary,

lawyer, accountant, hairdresser, dressmaker, manicurist, maybe a therapist, also maybe a masseuse—but it wasn't an automatic fait accompli that each had his or her own personal trainer.

Okay, so my dog needed a personal trainer. I, who weigh 115 pounds more than he, did not have a personal trainer. But he needed one. They told me he required behavior modification. My little boy had not reached puberty yet, and already he was jumping on the ladies. Licking total strangers. Burrowing into those certain parts of me that refined ladies such as myself don't even admit we have.

They told me he lacked social adjustment. I looked at this furry, rumpled pile. Collars on my sweaters were bigger. And this was in dire need of behavior modification and social adjustment?

Listen, what do I know? I got him trainers. I was up to my eyeballs in trainers. I mean, I'm talking *trainers*. Woody Johnson owns the Jets. Sale Johnson, the mother of his children, is a champion horse breeder and owner. She has dogs. Her littlest one, BamBam, is a client of a star pet trainer who teaches things like, if your animal needs to poop and hasn't and you're, say, late for a plane and can't wait and you just have to make him do his thing pronto so you can get on with your life, insert the limp end of a paper match. It will cause sufficient minor discomfort that, to get rid of, he will exercise whatever must be exercised. Result? He'll end up doing his business.

Another star trainer is Bash Dibra, who now coaches possible co-op buyers on how to get their pets past the notoriously finicky co-op boards. Some apartment buildings in Manhattan won't take canines over twenty pounds. Presumably, prospective residents starve them before the board meeting. I only know that Bash then coaches them on manners. I mean, God forbid your chihuahua should do his thing right on the board chairman. It could cost you a duplex.

Another trainer, I was told, charges $750 for a consultation. For that money, I told him, I'll get down on all fours and bark myself.

I had one trainer come in and interview *me*. He lives on Long Island and to park his car he charged me $65. I said he either takes the train next time or he finds himself another client.

Celebrity trainer Warren Eckstine is widely known from his appearances on the *Today* show. He and I were on NBC-TV together for years. Every Saturday morning forever and ever he and I shared a dressing room with his dogs, cats, birds, snakes, iguanas, turtles, reptiles, rabbits. He writes books and once wrote that every time he came into the studio with a new variety of creature, he'd find I was already wearing it.

Warren, who lives in California, made a house call for me and pronounced my animal absolutely perfect. Said Warren, "Nothing's wrong with Jazzy that having another owner wouldn't cure."

"What's that mean?" I asked.

"It means a pet takes on its owner's mannerisms."

"Which means what? My dog's going to write a column and wear fake eyelashes?"

"No. Means he's just not a laid-back dog. He has attitude and expects a lot of pampering."

"What are you saying, that I'm not well adjusted?"

"No. Just that he's Cindy Adams's dog."

"I've known you a long time, so I'm going to take that the nice way," I said as Warren raced for his plane.

Everyone had a trainer with a résumé and credentials up the kazoo. I've since determined there's no such thing as a noncelebrity dog trainer. This one tells you he trained so-and-so's Lab. That one tells you he trained such-and-such's greyhound. I was very impressed with them all. Meanwhile, my beauty was slowly training *me*.

When he whimpered, I came. When he barked, I ran. Since I was working all hours and paying all the bills and supporting the whole household and handling every non-stop problem, I stupidly thought I should have some peace once in a while.

All I really wanted was for Jazzy to follow the command "Ssssshh," so I could maybe sneak him into a relaxing movie. Not that he was a Meg Ryan or Johnny Depp fan or anything, but I adore going to the pictures. I don't mean VIP screenings. I mean the neighborhood theaters. And I wanted to take Jazzy because I loved doing this, too. I wouldn't expect him to sit through anything violent or noisy. Nothing that would make him react negatively. Unfortunately, I couldn't find any neighborhood place still playing *The Sound of Music,* so for my first try I settled on *Bridget Jones's Diary.*

I deliberately picked the last showing, late at night, when the theater would be less crowded. In the middle of the movie, about where Hugh Grant and Renée Zellweger were getting set to do what boys and girls do whether they're terriers or humans, Jazzy started gasping. It was loud. It sounded like a reverse sneeze. And it didn't stop.

I ran out of there and got him home. I put him on my lap to comfort him, but he continued gasping, only it now seemed even more severe. As though he were choking. For sure something terrible was happening to him, something I myself couldn't fix. Although it was now the wee hours, I woke up a vet who had a surgery close by. I explained it was an emergency.

I grabbed a cab and raced to the vet's examining room. He was already there looking somewhat askew, having obviously gotten up from bed for this emergency.

I said, "Maybe something's stuck in his throat. Maybe a piece of popcorn."

We put Jazzy on the table.

This dog instantly stopped gasping and choking.

As the vet examined him, the dog looked up at us both with this odd expression as if to say, "Who? What? I'm fine. What is it with you?"

The vet looked at me the same way and said quietly, "I see nothing wrong with this dog."

My terrible life-and-death tragedy having fizzled, my dog, clearly not on the brink of death, was quietly nuzzling me.

I didn't know what to say. This was a replay of when my TV began sputtering and I demanded the repair people take care of it instantly. No, next week wouldn't do. No, tomorrow wouldn't do. It had to be today. Now. And when they finally made a special dispensation and dispatched one of their techies, who came over after hours, the damn thing hummed like it was Sinatra.

I apologized to the vet. There wasn't a whole lot a person could do to ameliorate the situation. I said whatever it is you could say under the circumstances and slunk home.

I hailed a taxi. I clambered in. The driver took off. My dog started gasping and choking.

I picked Jazzy up. Holding him nose to nose, I stared straight into his eyes. I didn't blink once. And I said right to his face, "Look, I don't know what you're trying to prove, but I'm telling you now you are not going to win. I'm going to bed."

Boy, did I need a trainer.

My lawyer is Barry Slotnick. His clients segue from New York's famous Subway Gunman Bernhard Goetz to the equally famous crime boss Vincent "The Chin" Gigante, who for years stumbled around in a bathrobe talking to himself. Slotnick suggested I hire Ivan, with whom he had worked when his own dogs had hang-ups several years before.

Ivan, I discovered, had trained the four-legged fighters of the Israeli Army. This I thought was admirable but, just maybe, a little too much qualification for my little puppy. The simple truth is, we're not talking a killer attack dog here. We're talking something the size of Billy Joel's beard. Which takes a nap every day in the afternoon because its tiny heart gets tired.

Ivan explained that the way Germans teach dogs not

to go where they shouldn't is to put tacks down in the verboten areas. I explained that I wasn't interested in him explaining anything more to me and, in fact, my interest at that moment was in showing him the door. Ivan told me the fastest way to teach my dog to "heel" was to put a choke collar on him.

I told Ivan I'd heard that Russian bears who perform in the circus learn to "dance" when they're forcibly placed on sizzling hot floors. I also told Ivan I wasn't interested in my dog working for Ringling Brothers or in winning any Six-Day War.

Ivan subsequently shrank his teachings down to my level and we went to work. And with him I inched my way out of trainer hell.

He quieted Jazzy down sufficiently for me to attempt to smuggle him into my favorite restaurant. Le Cirque, where the elite meet, is the corner luncheonette for folks known by their first names, as in Calvin, Paloma, Bianca, Dustin. It's where gents like the Duke of Marlborough dunk their carpaccio in their shallots. Where H. Kissinger vacuums up his usual fish and veggies, and Princess Stephanie does venison medallions and gratinéed calf with Armagnac—whatever that is.

I knew that the owner, Sirio Maccioni, did not allow pets. He didn't even allow two-legged animals without ties. But I thought that if Jazzy kept his snout shut and didn't bark a word and just crouched in my pocket, it would work for everyone. Besides, I'd seen Soon-Yi Allen there eating with her fingers—she picked up a chicken bone in her hands and tore at it. I figured if Woody's young beloved could do that at Le Cirque, so could mine.

The problem is that I must have a hole in my lip because, somewhere, a lettuce leaf covered in salad dressing either dribbled off my fork or out of my mouth. It hit the floor. Jazzy was also on the floor. Later, when nobody was looking, I picked him up and put him on my lap. He honored me by placing oil and vinegar and tarragon with a dash of bleu cheese paw prints on my red silk designer suit.

I quickly stuffed the perpetrator back into his carrying bag and, to make the stains look undoglike, ran the prints together with my finger. It wasn't a big stain. It was a small, light stain. But everyone became concerned. Everyone helped. Bill Boggs of the Food Network poured water. Soap star Robin Strasser, who was at the table, tried club soda. A waiter rubbed it with cleaning fluid.

Such wetness widened my lap's tiny spot. I was now wet from waist to hip, around my behind, dribbling down the hem. To sop up this bright red puddle, the maître d', directed by Sirio, dumped talcum on me.

This bedraggled designer rag was sent to the cleaner, who had no trouble removing the spot. He went right for the scissors.

I refused to give up. I also wanted to be able to smuggle Jazzy into church. He needed to be taught only to obey the command "Ssssshh."

Karen's for People + Pets is a Manhattan emporium that services the city's blow-dried, glorified, dandified dogs. She was perfecting a handbag carrier that didn't look like a Sherpa bag or an obvious doggy crate. It looked and, in fact, was, a regular shoulder tote but, unknown to the outside world, it also could secrete a dog.

This way, on a Sunday, when I'm alone and he would be all alone if I went out, I thought I could transport him inside for a church service unbeknownst to the ushers. And if he learned the "Ssssshh" command, I'd have it made.

On our first tryout I was so nervous I couldn't concentrate on the service. To limit the amount of time inside the sanctuary, I planned to arrive just as the first hymn was being sung. With the congregation standing, with the sound levels high, I felt there was a better chance of sneaking into a back pew and getting him settled.

Ten minutes later, in the dead quiet that followed the announcement of silent prayer, there came a short but unmistakable woof-woof. The parishioners looked around. Not knowing what else to do, I followed their lead. I also looked around. When they *tsk-tsk*ed and shook their heads uncomprehendingly, I also *tsk-tsk*ed and shook my head uncomprehendingly.

One lady with blue hair arranged carefully inside an almost invisible net met my gaze and mouthed the words, "Did you hear barking?" I looked back at her and mouthed the words, "I can't believe it."

I figured that's no lie. I'd hate to break a commandment in church. It could ruin the raise I'd been praying to get from my paper.

Meanwhile, I quickly found a treat and stuffed it in my animal's mouth. He flopped down again quietly.

The problem was the soloist. It truly was an assault on every kind of ear. Not just my dog's pointy ones. She was a quickie replacement that Sunday. Not that she was bad, but put it this way: It sounded like someone was tearing a dishrag. Jazzy, whom Warren Eckstine says has taken on my coloration, cannot bear mediocrity. And a loud, flat soprano is more nerve-racking to him than a Siamese in heat. He jumped from my lap and took off down the aisle.

Thank God he's low-slung. With my head also down low as I lunged after him, the few worshippers who mentioned it later told me they thought my hairpiece had dropped on the floor.

CHAPTER 8

Mother's Day

The storefronts were filled with Mother's Day. The newspaper ads kept telling you what to give your mother. All I could give mine—whom, from the day I was born, I loved more than anybody else in the whole world—was a gentle, easy, slow-moving hug. One that wouldn't frighten her. One that couldn't be returned or even understood. My adored mom, who has forever been the very core of my life, no longer knew who I was.

I was brought up an only child. I never had children of my own. All of my life I have had only two people who meant the world to me: my mom and Joey. My mom, Jessica Heller, was a stunning, bright, sassy redhead. An executive secretary who won awards as the fastest typist in the office. Her wit and sense of humor made me want to be like her when I grew up.

My husband and my mom were the same age. A lifetime ago when I was married, I made a joke. I said, "When time comes for a nursing home, my husband and my mother are going to go together as a package deal." Forty years ago it was a joke. It had about become reality.

For decades my mom and I lived one block apart. In the good years when it was the four of us, my mom, my dad, my husband, and me, that block was traversed a hundred times a day. Even by phone that block was crossed ten times a day.

And then there were three. My dad was the first to go. A hired companion helped fill Mom's emptiness and I remained only a call for help away.

Now my husband was gone six months. And she'd moved. Home for my mom became a private house in the Hamptons, which I maintained with loving people to watch over her. I made the journey there regularly. Sometimes I stayed overnight, sometimes for the weekend or a few days, sometimes I drove out just for a quick bowl of soup and kiss on a cheek.

Our relationship, our love, our caring for each other

are the most priceless gifts God could ever have given me. When I was little, I needed her. And she was there. She gave me three-cornered little green tablets called Feosol. They were iron pills because, supposedly, I was anemic. That bottle was always on top of our refrigerator, and I always got them. Even when she had to work she'd call whoever was minding me to make sure I got those pills.

Then I grew up and didn't need her to do for me. But *she* needed *me*. Her needs were on top of *my* refrigerator or desk or mind. Whenever she was in need of help, whether trivial or of monumental proportion, she knew—when she was still able to know—that I was there. I'm not saying I was always patient. I'm saying I was there. Only a heartbeat away.

Mom did everything for me. My husband said she even helped make him marry me. She gave me dramatic lessons, elocution lessons, makeup lessons. She taught me about the birds and bees and guys. She walked me through My First Time. She got a diaphragm for me. She was always there for me so I never had to be embarrassed or frightened to ask her anything.

And then came the time she had to ask for help. And she was embarrassed and frightened at how often she found herself asking. And it was the kid's turn to give the mom that total sense of protection.

For a while I tried keeping a semblance of life around her. I took her to the theater until she started talking back to the actors onstage. Fortunately, there were certain friends to whom I'll always be grateful. Like Angela, who owns Pennyfeather's in the Village, and would invite Mom and make conversation with her. Like Tommy, who'd take her to the famous theatrical hangout Sardi's for lunch on matinee day, when the restaurant was its busiest. She'd see life. The handpicked people we invited to fill out the table would look away at signs of the ravages nobody should have to witness.

Until just a few years ago when she was no longer able to travel, I'd send Mother and a companion to Florida for a few months every year. Since she was growing forgetful, a gate surrounded our Florida property so that she was safe and would not wander off. The last winter she went there, accompanied by Tommy, the gate became unlocked the day they arrived. There had been heavy traffic in and out of the property.

Mom happily walked through it and out into the beyond. The authorities went searching for her, bulletins went out for her, Tommy went wild looking for her.

Joey and I were in New York. We had no idea what had just happened. She had only that morning gone to Florida and, in fact, Joey didn't even know she'd left.

Hours later when the police reunited her with Tommy, the electrodes in her brain were in the off position. She did not recognize Tommy. He was in the odd position of saying, "This lady is in my charge," while she was saying, "I never saw him before in my life."

So the cops called me. Joey answered the phone. They said, "We need you to identify a woman who seems to be lost. Can you tell us the whereabouts of your mother-in-law?" Said Joey, "Of course. She's one block away from me in Manhattan."

They arrested Tommy.

Fast-forward. It was now a couple of years later. It was the first Mother's Day that I felt truly alone. I not only didn't have the mother I'd known all my life, I also didn't have the husband I'd had for forty years. There was a shaky, chilly feeling inside my gut as I drove out to hug my mom, spoon-feed her a little hot cereal, and, maybe, sing a favored song to her in hopes it would spark something.

I took Jazzy with me. "Jazz," I said to him, "you're only blood relative. The only family I have left to call my own."

His sweet face seemed to show he recognized what was being said. He licked my eyes.

I stared at him and realized I'd become a truly crazed,

demented mommy. And, like any other, I swear no child is more beautiful than mine. WNBC-TV's longtime news anchor Sue Simmons also has a Yorkie named Jazzy. But, I thought, hers is some gargantuan tubby of seven pounds. Nothing like my slim, beautiful child.

"Jazzy-poo," I said, "you're it, baby. Nobody to love and to love me except you. You're all I have now."

I put him in the car with his CARE package. Toys, treats, travel water bottle, puppy papers, plastic bag, and paper towel should this carpenter of mine decide to do an odd job on the way. In the old days I had to pack up for Joey. His medicines, special foods, special needs. Now instead of Joey it was Jazzy. Different stuff but, still, a CARE package.

Jazzy wriggled around until he found his position. He scratched at the leather seat with his front paws, making absolutely no change anywhere but, ostensibly, making his resting place comfy. Eventually he curved right into my thigh and never moved. He snoozed quietly for the whole two-and-a-half-hour drive. When we arrived I rumpled him and cuddled him. "Such a good boy," I said. "I love you."

Jazzy's language skills had expanded. He wasn't enrolled in Berlitz or anything, but he seemed to fathom the word "love." I elongated it, as in "I *looooove* you." Presumably the word soothed him because, when he heard it, he wobbled away contentedly.

The house was cozy. Lunch was being laid on the dining room table. The live-in caretakers, Judy and Scott, greeted us both with hugs and kisses, and I went off to my mother's room. My mother's friend Tommy was also visiting. The TV, as always, was on. Just to break the eternal stillness. Her eyes, which didn't appear to be taking any messages back to her, were turned toward the cartoons.

Mom's legs curled. They were no longer straight. Pillows were propped under them. Judy had placed a light blanket over them. Scott had rouged her cheeks. For one quick moment, I let down the hospital bed rail and came right up close to Mom and kissed her. There was no smile, no reflex flash of recognition. No word. You could see only that she had no fear. She could apparently sense that this being who was hovering over her was a friendly being. Somewhere in the lost recesses of her mind she knew, intuitively, that mine was a friendly spirit.

I wanted to crawl right into the bed alongside her, but there was no way. No room. And I was terrified I'd frighten her or cause her discomfort. Worse, that the bed would collapse. And so all I could do was stroke that small head. It appeared to me it had gotten smaller. I remember that head when it was full of information and was big and strong and featured that powerful mane of thick reddish hair. It seemed now tiny. The hair white. Sparse. Shiny.

I leaned in close, my body flat against the protective side bars of her hospital bed. I stood there stroking her and repeating over and over, "Mommy, it's Cindy. It's your daughter, Cindy. It's me. Cindy. Mommy, darling, I'm your daughter who loves you. I'm Cindy. You know Cindy."

And Jazzy went nuts. He was usually okay as long as I was nearby and he could see me. He was in Mother's room right with me. The door wasn't shut behind me so it wasn't as though he was closed out. He was smack in my sight line, staring straight at me and playing contentedly with his toy a few feet away.

As I leaned over to kiss my mother's face, he began to bark like a wolfhound. And wouldn't shut up. The more I stroked, the more he barked. This animal, which had been so pliant and soft and cuddly and silent and contented for two and a half hours, was now a board-certified wacko. The damn dog barked crazily. Baying like a wolf, he was.

I left my mom to see if there was a problem. Had he stepped on a pin? Had somebody accidentally placed the vacuum cleaner on his tail? No, he was fine. He wasn't even being ignored. Others in the house had been paying him mind.

I patted him. His tail began to wag. And I went back to my mom. I started to feed her a little cereal. The minute I put the spoon from the bowl to my mother's lips, Jazzy went nuts again. He jumped from the floor to the daybed on the other side of the room, faced us, and barked nonstop like his life was in danger.

I walked over to soothe him so he didn't frighten Mama. I picked him up, hugged him, petted him, told him I loved him, threw his ball so he could play fetch. At last, he was silent and happy again.

I left him to walk the five steps back to Mother's bedside, and Jazzy went bonkers again. Barked and barked and barked.

I continued to talk to my mother, but I had to raise my voice to be heard over the cacophony of sounds coming from a few feet away. Tommy, who was three rooms away, shouted, "The dog's barking."

Like I hadn't known it myself. I shouted back, "I realize that."

The healing quiet that had been wrapped around my mom was now broken by barking and shouting. Boy, was my visit becoming a pleasure for my mother.

"Stop his barking," shouted Tommy from his bedroom. "He's barking!"

"I know he's barking," I shouted back, my lips directly

at my mother's eardrum because I was kissing her sweet head. "What the hell do you think I think he's doing, whistling 'Dixie'?"

"So take him out!"

"Out? But my mother's *in*. Considering the drive round-trip is five hours, you think I'm going to spend the time *not* with my mother?"

Jazzy was still barking, Tommy was still hollering, I was still shouting, and my mother's eyes moved from me to the dog.

Jazzy had jumped onto the sofa bed, which was against the wall across from where Mom lay. He was positioned at the very tippy-tip end of the sofa bed. He was standing at attention. Facing us. And barking nonstop.

I took him in my arms and made soothing little sounds until he calmed down. I was determined to make this work. Holding him tightly, I put him near her.

Jazzy nuzzled Mom politely, but then he began forcefully licking her. I was so worried he'd frighten her in his excitement that I pulled him off and sat him on the chair next to her bed. In one shot he vaulted smack back onto the bed and made for her face. My mother's eyes widened. I grabbed him with both hands and plopped him on that sofa bed across the room. The instant he was back on that sofa bed the barking began.

"He's barking again," came Tommy's unnecessary shout from the other room.

"Shut up," I shouted back.

"Take him out."

"And what should I do with my mother? Also take her for a run in the garden?"

"Take . . . the . . . dog . . . OUT!"

"*You* take him out."

"I don't want to take him out. I have a cold."

So I took him out onto the deck. We played fetch for a solid fifteen minutes. I then had a long talk with him. I explained my mom wasn't well and she needed me and I wanted to give her a little comfort and it didn't mean I didn't love him. I did love him. I *loooooved* him. But for the next hour I needed also to love my mother and then, right after that, he'd have me back again.

Jazzy's hearing is A-one perfect. In New York City, with the television on, he can hear our astronauts in space. But this time he did not hear one word I'd said. I brought him back to the sofa bed. Went back to my mom's side. He went back to barking.

This was like Joey's jealousy. Joey always needed to talk to me about something urgent—like our will, like our taxes, something vital and private and that absolutely needed to be discussed That Moment—whenever my mother was around. I sighed deeply. Joey . . . Jazzy . . . Jesus!

I'd brought my mother a big huggy teddy bear. A red one with a luscious bow. Geriatricians had suggested she have something soft close by to cuddle so she didn't just have those cold, hard iron rails to lean against. So she'd always have something fuzzy and crushable to feel, to curl her fingers around, to touch.

It was in a bag. I took it out and placed it at my mother's side. I first snuggled it up against my own cheek to show her. I smooshed it in my arms and kissed it and rubbed it to show her. Wrong move.

Jazzy went ape again. He stood up en pointe and went, "Ggggrrrrrr." To straighten Mom's coverlet I removed the teddy from her bed. I put it on the floor. He went for it like Yasser Arafat for Ariel Sharon. He grabbed it in his teeth and shook it side to side, fiercely slamming it against the furniture. This heretofore sweet little puppy was bent on total destruction.

I grabbed him up and shoved him firmly under my arm. I retrieved the bear, shook it out, wiped off the slobber, and returned it to Mother's side. I faced the fact that my darling was spoiled. I wasn't strict enough. I was too indulgent. But I didn't really want to pen him up or thwack him with a rolled-up newspaper or holler at him or rub his nose in stuff or rattle a can with pennies in it so it scared him or let him bark incessantly until he exhausted himself.

I love him. I do not want to do any of those things. Kill him, yes. Discipline him, no.

I finally closed Mom's door, went into the dining room, and found myself a chair. Jazzy snuggled onto my lap. Having worn himself out, he snoozed there peacefully. Me, I collapsed.

CHAPTER 9

A Day at the NYP

Although I write a column for the *New York Post* six days a week and have been with the paper twenty years, I work primarily out of my own offices and don't go down to its headquarters often.

But one day I dropped in. And I brought Jazzy. Dogs aren't allowed in the building, but I had a legitimate reason for sneaking him in. There was talk that Jazzy should write a pet column. His opinions on doggy affairs, his comments on the celebrity animals he plays with, his take on having me for a mother. So I wanted to bring this budding journalist of mine to meet his colleagues. Besides, I figured it's time he saw where his mother worked. I bathed him, brushed him, perfumed him, dressed him in a red jeweled collar so he wasn't ashamed in front of the neighbors, and carried him into this heartbeat of the City of New York.

Arriving at the *New York Post* offices early in the day is the same as walking into a condemned building. No one's there. I arrived so early that the security guard on duty had never even seen me before.

I was well prepared for my surreptitious entrance. I was carrying a custom-made shoulder bag. Inside was a doggy carrier. Outside were special zippered compartments that served as my own personal handbag.

I owned two of these specially designed shoulder bags. A cuddly cashmere-lined fleece job for winter, a black patent for summer. Now when I carted Jazzy with me, I was not encumbered with two bags.

My hand—the one that wasn't touching Jazzy in his carryall—gave the fellow on duty a royal queen of England wave as I sailed toward the elevator.

"Yes?" said his voice.

"What yes?" I said.

"Where you going?"

"The City Room."

"ID, please."

"ID? What do you mean, ID? I'm Cindy Adams." That ought to shake him up, I figured.

I figured wrong. The one shook up was me.

"Your ID, miss." Even the "miss" didn't redeem him.

"Look, open your *Post*. My picture's been there almost since Alexander Hamilton founded this thing."

"I need ID."

I looked around, but there was nobody to help me. I set down my all-purpose shoulder bag and unraveled the leash, which was twisted around my wrist under my sleeve. While the guard calmly read the newspaper—*not* my column, incidentally—I squatted on the floor and began pawing through the bulging sack. I couldn't upend the thing and dump out its contents because my dog was its main content, and if this guy wasn't going to let *me* up, I figured I didn't have a really fat chance with a dog who wasn't allowed there in the first place.

In addition to two of his toys and a plastic bag in case Jazzy got jazzy, I had in my own personal zippered compartments a mini-tape recorder, which was broken from having been banged around, and a week-old invitation pleading with me to attend an event I'd never attended because I could not find the invitation. There was also damp maroon ink, since my Mont Blanc had developed a bladder as leaky as Jazzy's.

But press card? No. From down on the floor my muffled voice reached the security guard. "This is ridiculous. I mean, I had dinner with the publisher Lachlan Murdoch and the editor in chief Col Allan last night."

Politely he replied, "Just doing my job, miss."

I found my Police Card, the one the NYPD issues working journalists so they can get through police lines in an emergency situation. He stared at the photo. "Doesn't look like you."

That was very insulting. The thing was only a few years old. "Well, call upstairs. Somebody will identify me."

"Nobody up there. Nobody to call. Nobody in yet."

From the elevator came one of the building's cleaning men in his professional blue overalls. "Oh, Mrs. Adams," he said, staring straight down at me on the floor. "Pleasure to see you. My wife loves you. She reads you first thing every day when she gets the paper."

"Thank you," I mumbled, speaking directly into his rubber-soled work shoes.

He bent down with a torn piece of paper napkin and the stump of a pencil. "Mind giving me your autograph? It's not every day I bump into you. So, tell me, what are you doing here at this hour?"

"Trying . . . to . . . get . . . upstairs." I bit off each word.

"Oh, she's okay," said the maintenance man in the blue overalls to the security guard. "I'll take responsibility for her."

❧

In the City Room, nothing was stirring, not even a mouse. Even those who theoretically report for work at 11 A.M. don't straggle in before noon. Our presses roll at 10 P.M. Lockup is 8:30. Unless a reporter personally knows that the Seychelles have declared war on the United States and the Seychelles are winning, he can't file a story later than 8:00. It's from the afternoon news meeting onward that the City Room, the heart of New York, is pumping.

The City Room is an open oblong the length of a city block. The far wall of windows displays a dazzling view out onto the skyscrapers and canyons of Manhattan. The near wall is a warren of glass-enclosed offices for the assorted editors. Here sits Steve Cuozzo, who checks me for legal problems, plus checks for repeats in case another section of the paper has a similar story. There's Joe Robo, who's involved in the actual planning of the news pages. It's Annie Akilina, who's in charge of the budgets, the arithmetic, the expense accounts. It's Jesse D'Angelo, who runs those reporters who cover the city. To the left in the news room is the photo editor, to the right the layout people.

It's a world unto itself. Phones ringing, copy boys running, people hollering, everybody eating. We're talking a floor-through ghetto with desks that look like slums. Stacks of old papers reaching back to the thirteen original colonies. Junk piled so high it takes on the semblance of sculpture. With all of us sending out all day long for all kinds of snacks, there are empty cardboard containers and abstract shapes of leftover food everywhere. Somebody had laid on my desk half a bagel with cream cheese on it. The cream cheese had a smudge of black ink. If ever they vacuumed the place they'd probably find Jimmy Hoffa.

The lifeline of the City Room is the team effort. Everyone's in everyone's face. Even your thoughts end up public. Voices shout out, "How do you spell 'rhythm'?" "Who knows the capital of Rwanda?" "What's another word for 'circle'?"

One of the editors looked startled to see me. "Why are you here so early?" she asked.

"I'm doing social work among the uptrodden," I answered.

Being at the *Post* always brought the memories flooding back. My husband's humor column, "Strictly for Laughs," had become a staple of the *New York Post* immediately after Rupert Murdoch bought the paper. I learned early that the Australians had great smarts but, because they were newcomers on the scene, didn't have well-developed Rolodexes. I'd point them in the right direction. With Joey there front and center, we all got to know one another and I'd help them with whom to call, where to call. As the years rolled on we not only got to work with one another, we also got to play with one another.

This loose relationship solidified when the Shah of Iran was in New York Hospital. Back in the sixties, when JFK had dubbed Joey our "Ambassador in Greasepaint," his show in Tehran sparked the beginning of several visits—in Iran and in the United States—between the royals and the Adamses. Eighteen years later, as the shah lay dying in New York Hospital, his twin sister, HRH Princess Ashraf, invited me to his suite to pay my respects.

The entire New York press corps was ringing that hospital. So eager were they for any sound bite that if they could have found a couple of part-time orderlies from another floor, they'd have interviewed them.

That night Joey and I were to dine with the *Post*'s then-editor Roger Wood. I called Roger to cancel, explaining I had to go to the hospital to see His Majesty. There was a thud at the other end of the phone. Roger, stunned, had about collapsed in a faint.

"Dear one," he said softly, once he recovered, "could you perhaps ring after you come home?"

I not only rang, I wrote a whole piece about the visit. December 1979, my first article—unpaid, I might add— in the *New York Post* was a page-one exclusive with the byline, "The Post's Own Cindy Adams." I officially became "The Post's own" two years later.

Benjamin Franklin had written a gossip column for the *Philadelphia Gazette* in the 1700s, so I figured if it was good enough for Ben then it was okay for me.

And now, twenty-four years later, I've lived under five editors in chief and as many changes of ownership. I've lived through my paper's scruffy days when VIPs surreptitiously read the pages tucked inside the *New York Times*, or with brown wrapping around them. I lived through that era when it looked like we were going under, and some of us took to the streets to stump for our juicy beloved *Post*. There's a photo around somewhere of me sitting smack on the rooftop of a *Post* delivery truck, my short legs and high heels dangling over its windshield.

I set my darling dog down on an open space I'd commandeered near my computer. Although it was still early in the hot-weather season, the temperature had shot up several degrees, and my armpits were becoming damp. I hate to walk around in sleeveless shell tops. I'm at the point in my life where, if I wave good-bye to someone, the upper part of my arm is still waving ten minutes later. So, promenading through the City Room minus sleeves is not my idea of heaven.

The problem being, it was stuffy inside. I took off the jacket of my black pants suit and tossed it across my desk. Jazzy, being unfamiliar with his surroundings, feeling insecure, and worrying that I might just take off and leave him, immediately took up residence on my jacket, positioning himself smack in its very center. Somewhere in that little Yorkie brain, he figured that if I were wearing the jacket when I came in, I would most probably be wearing it when I left—and so that's where his doggy ass was going to sit.

Myron, who's answered the City Room phone at the *Post* since the days of Coolidge, came by to throw a ball for Jazzy, hoping to amuse him. Myron is an animal person. He has one cat who requires a daily injection of insulin. Jazzy ran after Myron's ball. Myron threw it again. Jazzy again ran after the ball. Myron threw the ball a third time. Jazzy didn't run after the ball. Instead, he looked at Myron as if to say, "Enough already with the stupid ball. I ain't moving again." And Jazzy didn't. He instead returned to the center of my jacket and remained there en pointe as assorted colleagues came by to adore him.

Things seemed to be going so well. Who would have guessed that my insides were churning? I found myself looking into everyone's eyes as they wandered by. I tried to read their attitudes. Did they love dogs, did they maybe not like me a little bit louder than usual for my arrogance in bringing him?

This was familiar emotional territory for me. I'd just come off a long spate of looking into people's eyes. Not for love or approval, but for understanding. It's the way an anguished mother on a plane with a special child glances at other passengers when her child acts out. It's a call for compassion. A silent plea to please, please understand. This is how I gazed at fellow diners when I'd steer my seriously fragile husband to a restaurant table. I was used to this looking-into-people's-eyes gambit.

In Joey's final years, I always had my heart in my mouth. I'd pray silently, "Please don't embarrass us. Please don't voice your *'why the hell would she bring him in here'* thoughts."

I remember well a March of Dimes celebrity chefs' cookout at the Plaza Hotel. Joey was still going out certain evenings, but things needed to be choreographed. Was it an all-standup cocktail affair, or would there be chairs? Was it a long walk from the front door? Were there stairs to negotiate? Was the men's room handy?

This particular gala was extremely crowded. It was not feasible to navigate Joey through the crowds that were milling about, juggling varying treats on tiny plates. I needed to race around to talk to people, to gather information for my column, so I parked Joey on a makeshift seat, an upended wooden crate, in the Terrace Room.

At that moment, a short, fat, ugly pig—think Humpty Dumpty with sprayed hair and a brooch—exclaimed loudly so we couldn't help overhearing, "God, she's still schlepping Joey around."

Like a tiger defending her cub I sprang at her. "The day will come that I'm no longer schlepping him, but you will still *always* be a short, fat, ugly pig."

So when I brought Jazzy on his first trip to the office, I felt once again the constriction in my chest that signaled the old fears. When dear hearts picked him up and hugged him, I breathed a little better.

Because my motto was "Never let 'em see you sweat," I masked my anxiety, but the truth is, I was tense. I couldn't relax or do my regular work. I kept watching for fear Jazzy would bound playfully toward someone who hated dogs or he'd happily try to lick another who thought a puppy's wet tongue was disgusting.

I didn't want him to get in the way. It's a working environment. Everybody's on deadline. They can be friendly for two minutes. For fifteen, not. They can chuckle when a pet chews crumpled-up scrap paper. They cannot smile when he chews exactly what they're working on. As he selectively chose to do that day.

At one point Jazzy was so excited that he walked right through his water bowl and slopped up the whole floor. He followed this by shaking himself violently. It dried him off, but it splattered a prized exclusive photo.

And he wouldn't eat. I had to resort to game playing. Digging into the dry food packet I'd brought along, I threw two of his little Eukaneuba pellets in the air. He caught one, ran after the second, and ate both. And this way, running and throwing and crawling on the floor from the features department to the sports desk through to the news bureau and all the way around to the women's pages, I ran back and forth. Like this I succeeded in feeding him lunch.

But I wanted lunch, too, and Eukaneuba just doesn't do it for me. So I sent down for a turkey on whole wheat with mustard. I pulled out my wallet, which had two twenties and three singles. At that moment the phone rang. By the time I turned back, Jazzy was eating dessert. The dessert he was eating was my money. It was amazing how discerning my dog's taste buds were. He'd totally destroyed both twenties, but he never touched a single single.

CHAPTER 10

The Dirty Dog

J azzy had some unattractive social habits. One of them was sniffing up my dress. When he was still a baby and had only just come to me, he trembled so badly that Pat McGregor, who has the care of dozens of dogs daily, unzipped her blouse and plopped him inside to warm him and nurture him. Then came nighttime. We'd get in bed and he'd wriggle himself all the way up under my nightie. To tell you the truth, I don't know which of us enjoyed it more. Nonetheless, I fast realized that this had to be a definite no-no.

But Jazzy didn't limit his X-rated snuggling to nights. Even in daylight the problem was showing up. There's a low hassock in the kitchen. If I perched on it, before I could arrange myself comfortably, only a short docked tail was visible outside my skirt.

Ivan the trainer tried to break him of the habit. He kneed him: gave him a quick jab with his knee when he got too frisky and pesty with newcomers. Jazzy soon got the idea to behave. But when Ivan left, so did Jazzy's manners. I can just hear juicy Jazzy telling his friends, "The teachers will keep nagging you until you do what they say so you might as well do it. Play along so they'll think they've done their job and they'll leave you alone. But, and this is very important, you must then immediately revert to your old behavior, or your guardians will know there is no point in torturing you with more lessons. They'll be annoyed, but give them plenty of kisses and do your best cute act and they'll get over it and you can continue to do exactly as you please."

Jazzy's behavior reminded me of my first encounter with the actor Richard Harris, which took place many years ago. We were doing a radio interview, sitting across a table so narrow our knees couldn't help bumping. In the middle of my earnest questioning, Richard asked, "Are you married?" I said, "Yes." Then he asked, "Are you a fanatic about it?" I laughed and said, "Why, you old coot, you're a dirty dog."

Now with Jazzy I was beginning to think my young coot was a dirty dog. Clearly, my Fido was not gay. Men's private parts he didn't sniff. He was a lady's dog all the way.

I took Jazzy to an elegant Park Avenue society tea attended by that elite clique of wealthy socialite matrons who live to help Mankind. Or Animalkind. Any kind as long as they can be do-gooders. This group was raising funds for some esoteric cause like the Care and Feeding of the Endangered White Rhino of Tanzania. Suddenly Jazzy's whole body—except for the tail that was wagging like hell—disappeared under my dress into a triple-X-rated world. The dowager hostess's extended pinky finger almost curled around her cup.

A dog is always sniffing about. He sniffs other dogs, sniffs his food, sniffs his bed, sniffs the sidewalk, sniffs his master. I never actually understood how it works when he sniffs me. One day I'm doused in forty dollars' worth of perfume, another time I've been out in the hot sun and haven't showered yet. I don't always give off the same fragrance, so I don't quite know how that works. But Jazzy doesn't discriminate.

I took my dirty dog to Denise Rich's evening honoring Mikhail Gorbachev. Denise Rich, whose troubles with Clinton's pardon of her ex-husband, Marc Rich, made her front-page material, has everyone at her parties. She gave me permission to bring Jazzy. I brought Jazzy. He embarrassed me.

I am no delicate flower. Maybe that was Joey's doing because he introduced me to his let-it-all-hang-out world. The first time we met I was a teenage model doing my first radio interview. I'd just become some stellar thing like Miss Upswept Hairdo or something. Joey was doing a radio show with the boxer Rocky Graziano. Graziano said right into the mike, "That was some fuckin' fight the other night." This program was live. Joey said, "Rock, you're not supposed to use words like that on the air." And Graziano said, "Oh, my God, I'm some dumb son of a bitch."

Our first date was a celebrity-studded police benefit Joey was emceeing in Jersey City. It came complete with a motorcycle escort. Arriving there I went into the ladies' room as Tallulah Bankhead entered the next stall. She banged on the cubicle door and thundered, "Young girl, you in there, have you any paper?" I was terrified and there was no paper and I stammered, "N-n-no, Miss Bankhead. There's n-n-no paper."

Seconds later I heard a scrabbling in a handbag and that voice again shouted out, "Have you any Kleenex?" I hadn't. Silence a moment, then, "Well, do you have two fives for a ten?"

Joey's buddy Jackie Gleason lived in our building. In a penthouse decorated with red-flocked wallpaper. I'd never seen red-flocked wallpaper. Or a penthouse. Or Jackie Gleason in person. One evening Jackie rang our bell, said he was a little short, and needed a few. Joey peeled off $500. That same night Jackie—wearing the *Honeymooners* braggadocio that we all know so well— blew it all taking us to dinner and hiring a band to sere- nade us.

The first big movie star I ever met was Betty Grable. Joey was doing *Guys and Dolls* in a dinner theater. He was Nathan Detroit, Betty Grable was Adelaide. She said to me, this impressionable girl she'd never met before, "You know what I want for my sixty-fifth birthday? I've never been to Europe. I want to go over on the *QE II* and pay two men to service me the whole trip."

So, my rating on the shock meter ranges somewhere between zero and forget it. But that was B.J.—Before Jazzy.

At Denise Rich's dinner honoring Gorbachev, Jazzy began honing one of his less attractive social traits. In the center of the room, he rolled over, lay flat, and started to advertise. He'd been neutered, so why he had to show off his maleness in a crowded Fifth Avenue living room at the feet of Liza Minnelli I have no idea. My dermatologist, Fred Fenig, has an Irish setter whose male organ alone is longer than my whole animal, so what Jazzy's so proud of I haven't the foggiest. I only know he was out there flashing like he's Jack Nicholson.

One blonde in a mini had lovely legs. Jazzy liked them, too. His little tongue was traveling up her thigh before we could peel him off. Eventually, he took up a position on the floor and kept licking her toes. She gave him two "nice doggy . . . nice doggy" pats and he lay down quietly. While chatting with someone, she absent-mindedly reached down to rub Jazzy's head. What she reached was not his head.

In the midst of Operation Mikhail Gorbachev, I came to one irrevocable conclusion: I have a trashy dog.

CHAPTER 11

Don't Fence Me In

I wanted to have dinner parties in my new life, but I wasn't sure how to do it with this dog around. Did I lock him away? I didn't want him whining and barking and begging for tasties. I didn't want him eating people food. I didn't want him bothering the guests by jumping up on laps. To me, he was so delicious that if I could put mayonnaise on him I'd eat him but, still, I did not want him as a centerpiece.

I would sometimes stand back and just run my eyes over him. I'd stare at his tiny sleeping body, all curved into my side, his little breast heaving up and down. I couldn't believe how this small furry ball had wound itself around my heart. One starry 2 A.M I caught sight of him from the rear, silhouetted against the night sky. His pointy ears stood straight up, little strings of hair hanging off them. It was amazing to me that God had made anything so precious and lovable.

But this precious gem was wreaking havoc on my social life—which also happens to be my work life. When I was out I couldn't always concentrate on somebody's scintillating dinner conversation, because my thoughts were on this housemate of mine. My responsibility. My charge. I was all he had. When the hour grew late I was conscious that he was waiting for me. I knew he needed me. Who else would watch over him? Who else would care for him? I couldn't let him down.

Like one evening of back-to-back galas, one hosted by Graydon Carter of *Vanity Fair,* the other by Bob and Harvey Weinstein of Miramax. The Hubble telescope couldn't deliver more stars in one night. I scribbled away in my reporter's notebook, and when I finally felt glutted by celebrities, after I had enough notes to fill the next five columns, I went home.

You Know Who was not talking to me. He'd trashed everything. Flowerpots knocked over, newspapers shredded, Kleenex out of the box, pedestal under the table gnawed, ribbons on my baskets pulled, my bra and stockings were on the floor, papers I was working on were chewed, a ballpoint pen was destroyed, he'd eaten through a phone jack socket, which had been under a protective strip so he couldn't get to the wires. Scotch tape was entwined in his fur. I had two pillows from Afghanistan, embroidered with little mirrors on them. No more little mirrors. The Louis Vuitton case for my contact lenses was upturned, and he was playing with a silverfish bug.

He'd done a good job with our rubbish, too. There was a large black plastic garbage bag all tied up, knotted at the top, ready to be brought out to the incinerator and why it hadn't gotten there I'm still not sure. What I am sure of is that he made a swamp of it. He'd dug a hole in its side just the size of his mouth. Among its souvenirs had been chicken bones. There were now chicken bones distributed throughout the kitchen. And the perp himself? Sitting on his haunches staring at me with an "I didn't do anything" expression on his face.

It's a wonder how this small inarticulate being can be so filled with me, me, me. Take care of me. Pay attention to me. Play with me. Don't leave me.

Years back I had a girlfriend named Bernice. Bernice divorced a spouse for the same reason. I knew there was a lesson there someplace. I didn't know exactly what it was. I knew only that at least my dog wasn't cheating.

So a dinner party was a good idea. That way I could be in my own home while I was mining excellent mother lodes of information. Having a party in your home in some wise obligates your guests. And any reason for the event will do. Someone writes a book, someone else gives a buffet. Three Polish midwives emigrate to Staten Island, for New Yorkers it's a perfect excuse to do cocktails. This profession is all about sources, contacts, and networking.

Restaurants are impersonal. Your own home generates prime sources of material because those invited feel privileged. They've shared an intimacy. They then consider themselves close to you. That's what's meant by bonding.

House parties also alleviate the nervousness you experience when your pet is not feeling well and you have to leave him alone for a long evening.

His Excellency George Pataki, chief executive of the State of God-bless-us New York, was having a very informal, very intimate sit-down dinner. All together we were ten. Just close friends. In the Executive Mansion in Albany. All was pristine white. The table was laid in white linen. The tapestry on the dining room chairs, blue and white. Flowers white. China white.

I was antsy. It was a two-and-a-half-hour drive back from Albany, and I knew that when I had left my dog, he had been sneezing and wheezing. To cover my anxiety at this dinner party, I was holding court. My mouth was open. Naturally. If I'm not eating I'm talking.

All eyes were in my direction, possibly to determine if I would ever finish my tiresome, boring tale. With eighteen eyeballs fastened on me, I am walking to the table. I sit down. Still talking. Exactly, precisely as I sit, I make a sweeping gesture to accompany whatever interminable point I'm making. An oversized tumbler of red wine, filled to its fullest, is in my space. The oversized tumbler of red wine, filled to its fullest, goes all over. Over everything. Beet red, sopping wet, pouring onto the floor. It seeped to Newark. Forget the white table linen. My white silk lap, a pool of red. The silk too thin to absorb all the liquid.

Nobody knew what to do as I remained, stuck to the chair, in an ever-widening pond. To rise would saturate the rug beneath. I curled my hem, trying to contain the pool as though my skirt were a soup bowl, but the stupid sheath was too short and tight.

Staffers tried to blot my lap. Also, the height of indignity, stuffing towels under my skirt because I was dribbling through. Destroying the tapestry-covered chair of the State Dining Room of the Executive Mansion of the governor of the State of praise-the-Lord New York.

Forget the havoc wrought on the table itself. I was all-over magenta. I looked like a Fellini outtake.

Next major problem? What to do with me. How to haul me the hell out of the governor's house.

The Empire State's first lady gave me some of her clothes. Libby Pataki is tall, statuesque. Me, maybe a towering, majestic five foot four. I ended up with stunning black silk matelassé pants. But bunched over and over at the top and still puddling around my ankles.

Having destroyed the mansion, I finally marched out of the governor's life in his wife's wardrobe. It is my belief they were even happier to see me go than I was.

Of this I was certain: I had to do more entertaining at home.

It had been a while. I had stopped doing my own home dinner parties after one debacle years earlier. Joey and I had planned a sit-down to honor an impresario from Hong Kong who'd booked Joey a long time back. The guests were the impresario's star friends: Jan Peerce, the opera singer; Dong Kingman, the Chinese watercolorist; our friend Dr. Ruth. Ten in all. I prepared, we cooked, everyone fussed. It was winter, and the menu was shell steak and beef barley soup.

Jan and his wife were the first arrivals. "Sorry," Jan said. "Forgot to tell you. My wife and I are Kosher."

This was at 8 P.M. Straightaway I knew the shell steak had to go.

"But don't worry about us," they said. "We'll eat anything."

"*What* anything?" crabbed Joey. "We have no other anything and why didn't you mention it in advance?"

My housekeeper grabbed a can opener and my last can of water-packed tuna. Jan then peeped into the dining room. I'd personally set the table. It had taken hours. It was laid with antique Chinese porcelain. And he said, "Can't eat off your dishes."

"Ming Dynasty knows from dairy or meat dietary laws?" asked Joey. "Even if you went back hundreds of years, it figures the Jews were eating Chinese."

We had to scratch up paper plates and plastic utensils. The ones we found were green, left over from Christmas and always so chic smack in the middle of an elegantly laid blue-and-white table.

In came the Dong Kingmans. They were vegetarians. As in, no meat. This they announced upon arrival.

I knew we were already out of tuna. Other than a can of peas plus three onions, which we didn't consider a real main dish, we didn't have non–dinner party food lying around. We had no pantry filled with fresh veggies since we'd been out the night before and were dining out the next.

"Oh, don't worry about us," they said. "We'll eat anything."

Yeah, sure, right. Anything but what we were serving. We ran around borrowing from our startled neighbors. It was dinnertime. Joey rang the bell of a neighbor. He was holding a carrot stick. Joey pulled it from his hand.

Finally the Honoree arrived. Diabetic. He and his wife saw the noodle charlotte and homemade pie. "Can't eat any of this crap," they said.

The doorbell rang. Dr. Ruth. She was on the water diet.

None had told me their preferences in advance. So, then, why didn't they just eat bread or play with the food or go heavy on salad or hide the stuff in their pockets? I've been to dinner parties where the nouvelle was shrimp toes or grape grass or some hideous unrecognizable thing, and I just moved it around. Anyway, this was the very last sit-down party I gave during Joey's life.

I now resolved once again to give dinner parties. The world in which I live has a Noah's Ark mentality. Everyone travels two by two. Besides, just for career reasons, you need to keep up a social life when you're alone. And with my terrace, I thought what a lovely idea to give an outdoor dinner party.

One problem was the garden on the terrace. I thought of that nursery rhyme, "Mary, Mary, quite contrary, how does your garden grow?" About Mary, I don't know. About me, I know. Not. Roses, hedges, bushes, ivies, red maples, impatiens are supposed to grow, right? Wrong. With me they don't grow. I don't say they're not doing something. The weather had become so lovely that they were certainly doing something. In my case, rotting is what they were doing.

The year before, the nurseryman had planted evergreens. This year what I had were everbrowns.

Besides the gardening problem, there was Jazzy. He is only slightly larger than my hairbrush, but he has the gizzard of a cat. He's a jumper. In the house, cute. On the terrace of a high-rise penthouse, not so cute.

Indoors he'd jump from the floor to a hassock, from the hassock to a chair, from the chair to a windowsill. We solved that problem by moving the chairs far from the window and by screening the windows and by making certain they don't even open from the bottom but only from the top. This took engineers, contractors, glass people, building permits, and okays from our co-op board.

One lovely late spring day I took Jazzy out on the terrace. I was sitting at the picnic table having a cup of coffee and listening to the miseries of Diana Ross's people. A panicked secretary was saying to me, "You reported in your column that Miss Ross went to an off-Broadway show the other night. And that the curtain was held for Miss Ross especially because Miss Ross, you said, had to go to the ladies' room."

Jazzy had sprung in one effortless jump from the flag-stone floor smack up to the bench I was on.

"So?" I said into the phone.

The panicked secretary's voice was now so high that only Jazzy's friends could hear it. "As Miss Ross's secretary, I am the individual who always secures tickets for Miss Ross. I did not secure any for this particular show because Miss Ross never asked me to do so. Therefore it is not possible Miss Ross could have attended that performance."

Jazzy, bored with my being on the phone and paying him no mind, had now bounded airily from the bench right onto the picnic table.

I assured Panicked Person I had no personal interest in Miss Ross's bladder. However, I said, I knew for a one-hundred-percent fact that (a) she'd been there; (b) she'd been in the can; and (c) the curtain had been held for her.

Lining the outer rim of my wraparound terrace are wall-to-wall window boxes filled with shrubs and flowers and small trees. Each window box has a lip. Jazzy had now progressed from the picnic table onto the rim of a window box that, like all the others, teetered right on the over-hanging edge of the terrace. The terrace is ringed by a metal fence. Made for humans, not animals; there were wide spaces between its links.

I continued the conversation but rose from the bench. I was Sir Lancelot standing, nervous, half coiled, ready to leap. Whatever was unfolding on the phone in terms of Miss Diana Ross Herself was not really bothering me. My dog was creating extreme anxiety inside me.

I said into the mouthpiece, "Look, what is your problem? Is it that Miss Ross didn't go to this show or is it that Miss Ross doesn't go to the john?"

I don't know what her answer might have been because I could sense my dog was readying himself for another acrobatic vault into the air. I freaked. I threw the receiver down and screamed, "NO!" and grabbed him.

Thus began my odyssey in search of a safety net for my acrobatic pooch. I checked out chicken wire. A realtor friend had a terrace. Also a dog. He enclosed its sides with chicken wire. My friend Judge Judy has a penthouse, too. Also a white shih tzu named Lulu. Judy enclosed her outdoor area with chicken wire. My afternoons were spent with columns. My evenings were spent with chicken wire. My colleagues were mixing with the Mel Gibsons of the world. Me, I was inspecting chicken wire.

Lord, I was so busy. I tested it, worried the stuff wasn't sturdy enough because my dog could jump against it and knock it down. Then I tested an iron fence. Its points were like spear ends. A body could get hurt. Next up, a gate maker. He suggested a picket fence. Unfortunately, the vertical staves had enough space between them for Jazzy to wriggle through. Close the space and you ended with an almost solid wall that blocked the view.

I finally settled on a lacy, trellis-style barrier made of plywood. It wouldn't block the view and yet would be high enough so Jazzy couldn't get over it. Its crisscross pattern minimized the spaces Jazzy could squeeze through.

This took enormous time. And effort. A crew had to remove the existing window boxes and block-long shrubbery and sprinkler system and flagstones to anchor the trellis permanently. Then, just because this is Manhattan, the project required the permission of our superintendent, building manager, resident architect, staff engineer, in-house plumber, co-op board chairman, and the housing authorities. Then we had to redo the damn thing and take an inch off its height because someone considered it too high. Then we had to paint it white. Eventually the day came that we got the final okay and planned to replace the flagstones, window boxes, sprinklers, shrubs, trees, whatevers. This was the exact day Israel's prime minister, Ariel Sharon, picked to make a visit on our block. Below our building were Israeli SWAT teams in dark glasses, with Uzis, shotguns, rifles, Mace, and who knows what else—plus the NYPD, plus the Secret Service, plus various security people from the Israeli and American governments.

In the midst of this, crawling down our parapet, was the nice man who was anchoring my doggyproof trellis.

An Israeli sharpshooter on the ground, with my worker in his sights, yelled, "Freeze!" My guy, halfway down the stone facade of our building, froze. Legs dangling in the breeze. Israeli soldiers raced into my apartment. They flung my nice carpenter against the cement wall. They jammed a gun to his temple and frisked him.

Go tell these Mossad grads we're doggyproofing for an underweight Yorkie.

The way I figure it, doggyproofing my terrace cost me about eleven thousand dollars a pound—*and* a near-death experience. But now I could entertain.

CHAPTER 12

On the Road

Summer was approaching, and I decided to take Jazzy on the road. After all, he was happiest when he was with me. Or maybe it's just that I was happiest when he was with me. In any case, the idea didn't really work for us. I learned quickly what it means to have a dog's life. It means having a better one than my own.

It was in Washington covering a presidential event that I first determined room service doesn't cut it for my hound. Jazzy wasn't a big fan of vichyssoise for an opener and mousse for a closer. Nor did the minibar's beer, wine, and Toblerone do anything for him. He did, however, OD on the Lay's potato chips.

On the lower shelf of the television console the hotel had thoughtfully left a VCR and a *TV Guide*. My dog has selective dining habits. He ignored the *TV Guide* but he did eat partway through a cassette of *The Bridges of Madison County*. He retched afterward. "What's the matter?" I asked. "You thought the book was better?"

Eventually I ordered him a scrambled egg, which is one of his favorites. Plus his extraspecial treat, chicken liver. Unfortunately, you can't order a smidge. The cook doesn't know from smidges. Ask for the room service manager and you get a heavy French accent that sniffs, "Madame, we are cordon bleu chefs. Our specialité de la maison is langoustines avec des haricots vert, snails avec pommes de terre, and rack of lamb avec rémoulade. We do shrimp, we do sole, we do boeuf, we do poulet. We do not do smidge."

Right. So you have to order a whole dinner. The thing came with sautéed onions, a bacon strip, parsley, half a broiled tomato stuffed with breadcrumbs, and a side order, which I don't remember requesting, of creamed spinach. The whole deal cost me $65.

I offered Jazzy a spoonful. He wouldn't touch it. I tore off a few teeny pieces and with my fingers offered him a handful. He wouldn't even sniff it. Thank the Lord I like liver because, being cheap, I ended up eating his leftovers.

From now on whenever my doggy has a meal I'm going to have him bring me a people bag.

Canine behaviorists write articles that claim animals talk. Okay, I won't argue with that. But if that's so, I wonder why the hell mine doesn't tell me what he wants.

I ordered roast beef for myself so he could have a bone to gnaw on. He buried the bone. The maid turned down my bed, I went to sleep, I woke up in the middle of the night screaming. I'd been stabbed. I'd found Jazzy's bone. In my back.

Burying a bone? Why? For what reason? This is no mangy, grungy junkyard cur who has to bury a bone in some dirt pile so he'll have a snack for later. He doesn't exactly have to claw through brush and clumps to forage for food. He's hand-fed prime cuts and diced-up kosher chickens. His hand-painted water bowl is monogrammed. He lives on Park Avenue. He has a driver to take him on play dates. He attends bark mitzvahs and gets pawdicures. He is not exactly accustomed to rough-and-tumble. His silky fur is enriched with Keri lotion. His coat is fluffed and puffed and blown out with a hair dryer. He uses a designer doggy shampoo, which I had to go out and buy on this trip because it wasn't included in the hotel's Bulgari bathroom amenities.

The bell captain said that in his next life he wanted to come back as my dog. Yeah, me, too.

There were additional problems with the hotel's housekeeping department. I was out reporting on breakfast meetings, then a whole day of interviews, then a quick dash back to change, then straight out again to cover the parties. Because Jazzy was bored being alone, he unfurled the whole roll of toilet paper. The living room looked like a New Year's Eve gala. He was crazed, dancing around the vacuum, and his little tail, which is about the width of a caterpillar, nearly got sucked into it. He also barked nonstop at the mop because, to him, it was some strange sexy mongrel he needed to hump.

This being Washington, the hotel was very business oriented. Each room had its own fax. My killer attack dog had a pathological obsession with this machine. He lunged when pages spewed out. He shredded every document. VIP notes from the White House and personal correspondence I'd been desperately waiting for he destroyed totally. And this most angelic of God's creatures developed a fever when it came to devouring cover notes. In would come a five-page missive. Lotsa luck. Without the cover letter there was no shot as to who'd sent it.

Wagging his tail with all the energy his little behind could muster was enough to send the pile of paper flying

in every direction. Horrified, I wagged my finger at him:
"No . . . no . . . no."

And then I caught my reflection in the floor-length
closet mirror. Huge five-foot-four me shaking my finger
at this bit of fuzz who didn't measure as long as my amber
necklace. I thought, "What am I doing? They're going to
take me away."

Books tell you you're not supposed to feel sorry for a
dog, that he's a dog. He's not a human and he's not supposed to be a human. He's a dog. But every once in a
while I stare at mine. I think that he has no victories to
look forward to. I wonder what's going on in his head.

The truth is, he's smart. Like when I tucked his ball
under a tightly folded blanket. I watched the wheels go
inside him. He'd stare at it deciding to paw this way or
that. He'd weigh whether to make a certain leap or not.
He was always right.

He's smart about working me, too. In the living room
area of our junior suite was a maroon sofa with cream-
colored poufs. It still smelled new. I was just thinking how
lovely it was to have such a fresh decor when my precious
elected to mark it as his territory. I couldn't control my frus-
tration. I was crazed, since he clearly knew better and had
been doing things correctly and had just come through a
training session. I grabbed a rolled-up newspaper and

smacked it against the creamy pouf with a loud *thwack*. I shouted at him, then collected him and deposited him unceremoniously right inside the john door, where he was supposed to do whatever it was he was supposed to do.

Jazzy cowered. This little wiglet crept under the sink, head down, and trembled. And trembled. And trembled. He'd never known me to be rough with him before. He just quaked uncontrollably.

I was heartsick. I was overcome with remorse. I started cuddling him, thereby instantly undoing whatever punishment I'd exacted. The poor creature was getting conflicting signals, but I was so guilt ridden I didn't know what else to do. I couldn't bribe him. Couldn't promise him sex or let his sister come for a long-overdue dinner like I'd have done with Joey.

I looked at this little frightened thing. There's more hair inside my rat-tail comb than on his bones, and I was laying down the law to him? I hated myself.

One day later he was again on the sofa. Sitting straight up waiting for me. Suddenly he squiggled off and zoomed past the bathroom's open door, whereupon he rushed maniacally to the paper, which, as always, I had carefully spread out. He peed. But like a homing pigeon he'd zeroed right in on bin Laden's face. Then he just sat there waiting to be praised.

"Good boy," I said. "Good boy."

After my adored loosened the crocheted coverlet on the chaise and jumped up on the chambermaid and ripped her stockings because he wanted to play, she crabbed to me, "Why do you have one of these pesty little creatures? This thing just looks like an armpit. If you're going to have a pet why not have a *real* pet?"

I explained to her that you can't take a gerbil to a cocktail party, ferrets don't quite make the cut, hauling a Doberman pinscher into a tiny dressing room in a small neighborhood lingerie shop has its limitations, and keeping raccoons is against the law. The relationship of a small dog fits perfectly into the social life of a career person.

"A lapdog is to keep on your lap," I explained. "It's so you can snuggle with it. Its deliciousness is that it's portable."

"A Saint Bernard, now that's a *real* dog," she said.

"What? Please! Who wants some huge smelly beast with a lot of hair sharing your bed?"

"I'm single. Sounds good to me."

"Hey," I said, "I've already tried *that*."

"Well," she said, "I wouldn't mind."

"So get married," I said.

There was a good deal of wildlife on our floor because this was an animal-friendly hotel. It's just that the staff didn't share the feelings of the hotel. In the room right across the hall dwelt a cat who came with another of the journalists I knew. We often kept our doors open so we could run back and forth. I could see that the nice cat sipped from his saucer of milk and lapped up his cat food like a perfect gentleman. His name was Comfy. And that's what he was. Comfy with his food, his aloneness, and his ability to smoosh down on a car sack inside his mistress's angora sweater.

I yearned to take my Jazzmobile to cat obedience school. In fact, I yearned to take him to any obedience school. But I knew it would do no good. I had enrolled him in a Parent/Pet Class months back, and it did nothing. I learned to sit and speak two hours before he did.

Down the hall was Leo, a 105-pound Rhodesian Ridgeback. We met him in the halls because his master used to get a supply of ice cubes from the pantry on our floor and put them in his room fridge. Seems Leo was accustomed to getting an ice cube every night. One night his father neglected to give him his routine ice cube, so Leo tapped on the refrigerator door. I thought, "Oh, how wonderful to have such an intelligent, trained creature."

A Rhodesian Ridgeback is an African breed. Accustomed to heat. Bred to lope over rocks hunting lions in the scorching sun. Well, it was a 98-degree day. Jazzy, who's afraid of nothing, would play with an elephant if there was one available. A corridor that leads to the Presidential Suite is not the best idea for a dog run, but he jumped right onto this giant economy-size macho dog. It was sweltering. The air-conditioning in that wing of the hotel had gone south. The Ridgeback was panting. Lying down flat. Exhausted from the heat. Not exactly the kind of package you can pick up in your arms and place in an air-conditioned living room.

He ultimately crawled off and collapsed, heaving.

A Yorkshire terrier, bred in England, is not accustomed to heat. Nonetheless, Jazzy jumped and barked and hooted and cavorted and drove the Ridgeback crazy. I had to pack my tiny Yorkie up and take him back to our quarters. He was depleting this resident watchdog.

We were in Washington four nights. On the third, Jazzy won the Triple Crown. Full of attitude at being abandoned, he pooped right on top of the desk, peed in the freshly turned bed, and whoopsed from a piece of the dirty mop he'd chewed. I ask you, who needs to tip a chambermaid when you're doing full cleanup duty yourself?

My English Yorkie was keeping the room so dirty that I needed to hire a French poodle to come in once a week.

I was starting to not like this dog a little bit. This dog

reminded me of a guy I'd known a long, long time ago. I loved him. I was mad for him. I just didn't like him.

Parenting a dog was a lot of work, and the head house-keeper on our floor was not interested in doing it. One afternoon on the daily three o'clock round to see if everything was all right, she bent to check the minibar. Friendly Jazzy jumped up to lick her. She reared back.

I took offense. "They say a dog's mouth is cleaner than a human's," I snapped.

"Yeah? How about right after he licked his own behind?" she snapped back.

Our last night in Washington was built around a banquet. The table was set with commander in chief emblems—such as a Marine Corps cap made of shrimp, a naval anchor of cheese wedges, a White House built from chicken legs. The flowers were flawless, the silver was gleaming, and the ham as plump as Cher's collagened lips. All was ready. Just awaiting the VIP guests. Minutes before the arrivals I sneaked in to precheck things and give myself a heads-up on what I would be writing. I have no idea how, but my sweet pet, clearly a gold medalist Olympic broad jumper, had made it onto the table and from the table smack into the chicken-legged White House, which collapsed on top of him.

I ran back to the room to clean him off. He was a hapless, shivering mess and, besides, he hadn't had any food. I felt sorry for him. Despite his bad manners, I sent up an order of skinless, boneless roast chicken with a bit of mashed carrot and rice boiled in broth.

The door across the hall was open. Jazzy ran in. He ate the cat's food.

This hotel had shiny marble floors with center area rugs. The glitzy, glossy marble was spit polished. When my beloved ran up and down, his little back legs couldn't get traction and he spun around. Our final night, as I was packing, I allowed him out in the halls and he romped and raced and ran everywhere. Everywhere.

And slid into places where I never thought to look. Like into one foreign lady's suite. The night maid had hung a card on the knob saying, "Maid cleaning room," and had left the latch undone and the door slightly ajar while she was getting supplies. When my friends couldn't find Jazzy and couldn't shout for him since it was late at night, we peeked through the open door.

The bedroom was covered in snow. White cotton snow. Trillions of infinitesimal bits of white padding everywhere. Jazzy had methodically destroyed this lady's entire economy-size box of Tampax.

Covered in white fluff he then jumped into her open suitcase. We collected him and ran out before the maid returned. Thank God we found him, because this particular hotel guest was Japanese. If we hadn't invaded that bedroom, my dog would have been on his way to downtown Osaka.

It was summer and I wanted to try and take at least one vacation with my dog. But where? Friends planned for me to join them in Cancún until the travel agent said, "He could get sick from the food or the water or the atmosphere." Listen, in Mexico even humans can lose eight pounds on one lunch.

I didn't go there.

In France dogs are pampered. They're allowed into restaurants. Even welcomed. Since it was the season for the south of France, I entertained the thought of St. Tropez. That is, until another traveler told me of a hotel manager in the area whose German shepherd had eaten two Yorkies.

I didn't go there.

Paris, I thought. The couple I was meeting abroad was taking their Yorkie with them, too. But the stewardess ordered this couple's dog stuffed into his carrying case for endless hours and there wasn't sufficient air for him, and the captain said it was against the law to take him out.

I didn't go there.

I was deliberately forcing myself to become best friends with a person I didn't even like just because he had a private plane when a savvy Saint Bernard owner in Hollywood gave me a crash course in dogsmanship: "Fit Jazzy with a harness. Train him to operate as though you're sight impaired. Blind people are allowed to take their dogs on an airplane."

I said, "You nuts? Can you imagine Jazzy guarding anyone? I mean, Jazzy as a guide dog?"

"He doesn't really have to. He just has to take the course."

"Please. And I should pretend I can't see? What will I do when they start showing the movie—just listen to it?"

I mean, can you imagine having a Seeing Eye Yorkie?

The solution, I figured, was to stay in the United States and do weekends in the country. The problem there was that Jazzy, like his mother, was not heavy into suburbia. He knows from escalators, not azaleas. My dog knows the sound of garbage trucks, not crickets. His backyard is cement twenty stories down. The only birds and bees he's acquainted with are jewel encrusted and in gold and sell big in Tiffany.

It was the same with Joey. To Joey, New York wasn't a place, it was a religion. He was a devout New Yorker. He was born in our helluva town where there's a Chinese restaurant on every corner and you need an elevator to get to your pajamas. The man traveled everywhere, but for him it was New York. His quote? "Sure, New York has problems, but it's the greatest. We have eight million people in New York and some of them have never even been mugged once."

He didn't mind visiting a country as long as it wasn't *the* country. He'd go to the Arctic, just not to the Hamptons.

For decades I'd used Joey as my excuse for why I couldn't go to friends' country homes. With Joey gone, so was my protection. I now had no excuse not to go.

Therefore, at this stage of my life, friends reached out to invite me to their glorious summer houses. The point being, what good is having a fabulous pool and garden and private screening room and live-in couple and tennis court if nobody knows you have them? And to sweeten the experience, they all invited Jazzy.

So I went to decorator Carlton Varney's country place. He has some way-the-hell hinterlands boonies upstate farm in God-knows-where land. The place is 210 acres. Ponds, lakes, woods, deer, ducks. House dating back to the 1700s. I'm told George Washington slept there. For George, great. For me, not great.

The guesthouse, built before George ever made reservations, wasn't big with water. Carlton, who has decorated the vice president's house, President Jimmy Carter's home, the Greenbriar Hotel, and our Tokyo embassy, had his own lilac soap, pink towels, flowered sheets, and quilts handcrafted for him in Portugal. Nice.

But the toilets didn't flush.

I mean, no handcrafted Portuguese bedspread embroidered with the initials CV does the job when you really need a toilet that works.

The fridge in my quarters held champagne and caviar. Also nice. The problem was I was not in need of beluga with chopped egg whites. What I needed was a sink with running water. My dog was thirsty. Also I had to wash his food bowl. And there was still the little indelicate matter of going to the john.

This guesthouse lay deep in totally deserted woods. I was surrounded by darkness, forest, silence, major insects, and some black lake.

Suddenly, a big burly type with cut-off sleeves emerged from the bush. Kevin Costner he wasn't. The plumber he was. In my nightgown, with bear grease on my face—boy, was I not up to entertaining!

The plumber tells me the water worked before. Yeah? So? Lotsa luck. So did I.

He tells me the wells must've gone down and best I go

outside and work the pump. Work the pump? Outside? In pitch blackness? With only the noise of crickets who have insomnia? In some deserted jungle populated only by four-legged creatures in bushes? What work the pump? Work what pump?

Carlton eventually drove down from the main house in his pickup truck. What it usually picks up, I don't know. I know that this time I wanted it to be me. "No problem," says Carlton. "Just fill the toilet tank with water." I explain I'm a writer. I do daily columns. I do not do toilet tanks.

He takes the only glass around—a cranberry Baccarat long stem—and fills it with water from the pump.

He takes the white porcelain tank top off and pours in the minute amount of water from the glass. Then he returns to the pump and repeats the process until the tank is full. He tells me in case of emergency this is what I can do. I tell him what he can do. My dog is still thirsty. I offer Jazzy some of the trickle. He refuses it. I am reminded that, even if this were crystal clear spring liquid trickling down from the snowy peaks of Mt. Everest, he is used to Evian. Chilled, yet.

I have a thirsty dog, a cranky plumber, a testy host, and my own needy tummy. Carlton also owns a castle in

Dublin. He's invited me. I'm learning how to say "Shove it" in Gaelic.

Meanwhile, there's a charming pond on this property. In the pond is a beautiful swan. Despite its swimming around seemingly effortlessly, I knew that those gorgeous, graceful creatures can be mean and cranky. Especially if you encroach on their territory. There had been a story in the New York newspapers about a dog jumping into the lake in Central Park and being pecked to death by a resident swan.

I'm standing by the pond admiring this big, white, beautiful bird. My dog, who loves every living creature, plows into the water. The swan continues swimming. I'm watching carefully. It appears to be an idyllic, tranquil country scene. A pond, a swan, a dog. Sweet. Lovely. Pacific. And then I notice that the swan, which had been gliding in large circles around the perimeter of the pond, was imperceptibly narrowing its circles. Very slowly it was gliding farther away from the perimeter and closer to my dog.

My dog wanted to play. The swan did not. My dog was widening his horizons. The swan was protecting its domain. Jazzy, a happy innocent in this ecosystem, was being encircled. He wasn't a playmate. He was prey. I realized what was happening and dove in to collect my dog. I was splashing about, Jazzy was splashing about, the swan was circling. I screamed. A guard on the property then jumped in after me. This crowded pond now had a swan, a dog, a female, and a male. I grabbed hold of my wriggling dog and pulled him out.

The decision has been made. Jazzy's future travel plans will be to the living room and back.

CHAPTER 13

The Apartment

With Joey gone half a year I realized that while I was alone I was not lonely. And part of the not being lonely was having this demanding creature to care for. Except for the fact that you don't have to fight your way through a prenup, a Yorkie is just as much trouble as a husband.

Still, there were moments when the absence of Joey hit me hard. For instance, I had to fly to China. When I landed in Beijing, I had nobody to call to say, "I'm here. I'm safe. I'm okay." That's when you realize how alone you are. When you have no one to call from the airport.

The middle of the night when the surrounding world

is black was when the devil paid his visits. We're talking hobgoblin time. Thoughts spun round and round in my head, thoughts one should never remember. Like at the funeral parlor when the directress asked for my American Express card so she could charge Joey's cremation.

I blinked at her in horror. "You mean, you want me to get mileage on my husband's body?"

Death is a profession and she was a professional. She replied only, "If you prefer to pay by check, that will be fine."

There were moments when I felt I had to make a change. I was rattling around in an apartment that was too big for me. With Joey the place had been filled with home health-care workers, assistants, aides. Now they were all gone, and my house was too big, too empty. I started looking for something cozier. The kind of home you can pull around you like a warm blanket. I finally bid on a charming co-op that had lots of sun. I wanted it despite the fact that the board was not high on allowing dogs and would not consider any canine over twenty pounds. Even if razzy Jazzy was in the middle of a doggy combo, glued to the center of a Yorkie ménage à trois, the combined weight wouldn't equal twenty pounds. In any case, I yearned for this co-op so much that if he'd weighed twenty-one pounds, I'd have starved him for two months before I went before the board, and he could eat his first meal after we moved in. So, no problem.

No problem with me. The problem was with him. He did not like this building.

Jazzy gets negative reactions. I've taken him to my hairdresser appointments. I've taken him three different times, three different days, three different seasons of the year. Within fifteen minutes of each visit he whoopsed. Could be the aerosol cans of spray, could be the smell of hair dye, could be the snippets of ringlets on the floor, who knows. I only know he creates more difficulty at a beauty salon than Madonna. Result? He won. I no longer take him there.

So exactly why he reacted negatively to this high-rise, I haven't the foggiest. He did not take me into his confidence. I only know he sniffed it on the way in and turned his nose away like it was month-old Alpo.

Jazzy was summoned before the board to be interviewed. The chairlady was interested in his behavior around the perimeter of the property. She asked if we take him out for a walk twice a day. Walk? I explained his tiny legs have barely ever even touched the ground. He arrived via wheels, he travels via wheels. I explained I actually live in terror that someday somebody will communicate to him that what he's hopping into is only a sedan, not a limo.

I looked at this lady who asked me the question. "Walk?" I repeated. "Thank God he doesn't have to. *Walk?!* I mean, watch your mouth."

I said, "We *drive* him around the neighborhood. We don't walk him."

During this interchange my most angelic of God's creatures was sitting upright on his tail, front paws folded neatly in front of him. He was quiet, staring straight ahead, following the conversation intently. A person would have thought he was a graduate of Miss Porter's classes.

Although Jazzy did not need to submit a financial report, he did have to pass the board. They said they wanted to see his actions going up and down the lift and in and out of the lobby. So we took him outside. He was exuberant. One of his favorite playthings is a sneaker. Not a real sneaker. A rubber doggy squeaky play toy. Green colored. Well, my luck, this chairlady was toting a pair of green sneakers. Laced together, they were. As we chatted inside this super-high-class edifice, she set them down. Jazzy thought they were his toys. He began pecking at them.

This chairlady did not like dogs. She didn't like me,

either, so fat chance for a nervy Yorkie. Her pheromones must have given out that non-dog-lover odor because Jazzy returned the compliment. He sniffed around and his behavior quickly proved he did not care whether or not he fit this white-gloved building. This sly dog had already decided the building did not fit *him*.

Mrs. Chairlady had a dirndl skirt. Jazzy jumped up at her. Unfortunately, he'd missed his last manicuring appointment, and with the kind of long middle nail I would personally have died for he managed to scratch her calf. He then jumped high and his front paws lodged in her skirt's expandable elastic waistband. He pulled it halfway down her ample behind.

Not a good moment for a prospective tenant looking to make an impression.

After straightening herself out she bent low to wag her finger and growl, "Bad dog, bad dog." My bad dog compounded the felony by treating her South Sea pearls like they were Pop-its. He gave one good tug, and the pearls spilled to the floor.

When the pearls were collected, we walked across the street with the chairlady. Jazzy's nervousness had made him lose a little control. He isn't a wolfhound, so the package he delivered wasn't exactly the size of an end of roast beef or anything. It was more the length of a piece of penne. But, still. Fortunately for me, I thought, we were walking right past an open manhole. How convenient, I said to myself. Turned out not to be so convenient. Especially for the cranky Con Ed worker who then crawled up out of it.

When we made it back home he looked at me as though to say, "You knew I didn't like this place." He then gave me a Castilian bark that in dogspeak said, "Don't *eff* around with me next time."

My search for a new home was not going well. A friend suggested maybe I should consider a home on the Island, where I could take Jazzy for walks without fearing he'd be compacted by a garbage truck or swallowed by a pothole. So one Saturday morning Jazzy and I took a drive to the tip of Long Island. It was an exhausting day, schlepping through houses. By late afternoon I wanted nothing more than to go home. But just as I was getting into my car for the trip back to the city, my real estate friend asked for a favor.

I noticed then that she had a very harried-looking lady standing beside her. It seems this woman had no way to get back to the city that evening. She'd missed the jitney. Could I drive her?

Forget root canal. Forget Marine Corps basic training. *Real* hell is giving anyone a lift home from the Hamptons. Me, I do not want to be a caregiver anymore, especially for strangers. I want not to be pestered by smokers, coughers, talkers, or people with bladders like June Allyson's. I realize that's a bit antisocial. I realize I'm ripe for counseling. But, hey . . .

Maybe you like other people's kids schmearing runny chocolate on your car seats. Me, I don't. Not that I don't like children, understand. I just feel that if God had wanted me to have them in my car, he'd have first placed them in my womb. That's why I have a dog. Because I have no children. Another thing, a dog doesn't have luggage.

This person, who snookers me into a ride back to the city, then says, "I hope you won't mind dropping by my house since I have so much luggage." Luggage? Her behind was the size of a steamer trunk. Who said anything about luggage? I figured that's already enough baggage. She got in, and the Caddy sank down three inches. Even my shocks groaned.

And she's allergic to dogs. She looked at me beseechingly as she said, "They make my nose stuff up. They make me sneeze."

"My dog's only a few months old," I said. "He's too young to take a cab home alone."

Then, from some clump of bushes somewhere, darts this little boy. She'd never mentioned him before. I think she got him from Rent-a-Kid.

He climbs in. And right away he needs the john. We're not even on the highway yet. Why he couldn't have gone before, who knows? His mother points out the nearest gas station, which is, naturally, across a double yellow line on the wrong side of the road. Considering it was either a ticket or the upholstery, I had no choice.

I'm idling in early summer heat, killing my air-conditioning that already has a tendency to overheat my car, and watching three million other automobiles pile up on the highway in front of me while Mom's shouting to the kid, "Take your time, honey. Don't rush. No hurry."

Who's in no hurry? I'm checking my watch because I have an appointment back in the city and it's not with a pediatrician.

The kid finally gets in. Now my dog, who's long overdue by my calculations because he had a really nice lunch with little bits of hamburger thrown in, is getting pesty. I recognize he needs to go. I would normally have spread papers on the floor in the back, but there was no room because the passengers were there and they had some coats bunched up on part of the front seat.

I had to stop and take him for a walk. He became wildly enamored of some squirrel in the bushes and was no longer interested in his ablutions. I kept stalling and letting him play around in hopes he'd finally do what comes naturally. Unfortunately, it just wasn't coming.

The passengers were not thrilled sitting there while this dog chased a squirrel. The kid, sitting in the back, amused himself by kicking my seat. Scuff marks are not necessarily an asset to a brand-new car with six thousand miles on it. Two highway exits later this mother finally tells him, "This is not our own car, lovey, so better not do that. Auntie Cindy doesn't want it." Doesn't want it? Doesn't really like being methodically kicked and stomped? How about despises it? And them. And would wish to deposit both creatures by the side of the road underneath a tractor.

Jazzy was making whining sounds. I knew what those sounds were. I stopped the car and took him for a walk on his leash. Unfortunately, there was only the highway. I walked him up and down. Nothing happened. Jazzy's an indoor dog. He doesn't know about cement.

Back in the car we went since the passengers were making faces at one another. They were seriously annoyed with this waste of their time. Eventually Jazzy settled down and I drove them home and got them out of the car.

I wonder how long it took before they made the discovery. My very sophisticated pet, who has grown used to the best in life, had genuinely found the lady's cashmere coat to his liking.

Good dog.

After that experience I knew for a fact that I would not be calling the Island home. I want this? Houseguests? Junkets back and forth to the Hamptons? Overheating cars? Overheated passengers? No. All I wanted was my dog. Why was I complicating my life?

Hi ho, hi ho, it's back to the city I go.

There would be no move in my future. I did, however, need to make some adjustments. One was a security system.

I live in what's considered a safe area. But what can I tell you. There was a new neon sign on a telephone booth near where I live. It flashed, "Discover your world," for the Discovery Channel. The day after it was put up it was gone. Someone had discovered it. And swiped it.

And then not far from me there's this fancy building. A man parked his Lexus in front. Twice the windows had been busted and the car radio snatched. This time when he went inside to visit his girlfriend he left a sign on both sides: "No radio." He came out to find a scrawled message on the signs: "We know. We have the two of them."

And I myself reported on the dowager who'd bought herself a fakeola necklace. As she came out of Bergdorf Goodman's department store on Fifth Avenue, a mugger grabbed at her neck. This feisty lady pulled at the thing on *his* neck. Everybody screamed, everybody hollered, everybody ran. The upshot was, the mugger got a cheapo yellow metal and rhinestone job, and she got an eighteen-karat gold chain with a hanging cross.

Only in New York, kids, only in New York.

I figured you can't be too careful these days. That's when I called in my old friend Donald Trump. How old a friend? I knew him before he knew Ivana. I was at his first marriage and his second marriage. I was even around during both divorces. I'll probably be at his next catered separation.

How well do I know Donald? Before either of us was anything. Back when lawyer Roy Cohn was piloting him through New York's municipal kennels of power. Our very first meeting was a private dinner at the home of one of the city's prime power brokers. So prime that a few years later our host was indicted.

Anyway, at our introductory dinner we were seated

together. It was a round table for eight. Between us was the first of the endless beauties he attracts. Blond, eight-foot-long legs, dress cut so low that she'll someday develop chronic bronchitis.

And dumb? Donald leaned across her substantive front to say to me, "She'd have to ask for help to spell FBI." The two of us laughed from the fruit cup through to the baked Alaska and we've been close ever since.

So when I needed a security system I asked Donald for help—seeing as he knows all the experts who devise the protections that secure his buildings. His people set up an alarm system so sophisticated that if I get up to get a glass of water in the middle of the night, the cops come.

Hey, be it ever so humble . . .

CHAPTER 14

Prince Jazzy

Jazzy had now owned me for eight months. I sensed, however, that he was of the opinion that I required additional training. It bothered him if I didn't instantly play fetch when he brought me some scuzzy, spitty ball exactly at the moment I was conducting an overseas interview with a chief of state. He also seemed put out if I did not heel properly when he jerked the leash because, at that second, he chose to walk between a stranger's naked legs on the street.

I was aware that Jazzy, my closest living relative, was spoiled. An open can of half-eaten peaches on the third shelf in the back of a refrigerator with the electricity off isn't so spoiled rotten. Worse, this thing who has a stomach the size of a walnut so God knows the size of his brain, knows it.

Being the alpha male in this house, he believes he's the leader. One day he'll thwack a rolled-up newspaper on me to get me to understand he wants what he wants when he wants it. And does not want what he does not want.

When he really tortures me is Sunday. That's when he has me alone. If he doesn't have my undivided attention every minute of that day, he will express his displeasure. The Sunday papers are torn to bits. The plants he can reach are uprooted. The trash is overturned. His puppy papers get shredded.

And he'll give me the proverbial finger by refusing to eat. That's his coup de grâce. Refusing to eat. How in his doggy brain he can figure that his going hungry will harm me, I don't know—but guess what? He's right.

I wasn't Charles Dickens, my mutt's name wasn't Oliver, and my home was no orphanage. I couldn't bear putting him to bed hungry even though trainers repeatedly told me, "Do not coax him. Do not spoon-feed. If he won't eat, pick up his food bowl after twenty minutes. The next feeding time he will eat properly because he will be hungry."

Yeah, right. Easy for them to say.

I can't stand it. I recognize it's his way of getting attention. It's emotional, not anatomical. It isn't that he doesn't feel well. It isn't that he can't tolerate food. It isn't that his tummy is full. It isn't that he prefers a different menu. It *is* that this creature whom I just yearn to stroke and cuddle and kiss and love and hug and adore and coochie-coo is spoiled rotten.

Thanks to the Democratic Convention I actually learned that Jazzy is not my responsibility. The reason being, *he is actually the one in charge.*

The Democratic Convention was going to keep me busy for seven days. I figured this was a good time to give Jazzy special tutoring. We're not talking complicated executions. I didn't need him to audition for some Talented Dog segment on the Discovery Channel. I just needed him to learn certain commands like "come," "sit," "heel." So off I packed him to doggy camp upstate for special coaching. A hundred acres of outdoors filled with his own friends wagging and woofing.

Away I went to report on the red-white-and-blue rah-rah-rah-sis-boom-bah big masses with the big asses. And what, I thought, could be more wonderful in the heat of summer than to be exposed to more hot air.

Conventions are a week of hearing each pol, who'd earlier taken Bullbleep 101, answering each question with, "Glad you asked that because I'm the first one who proposed the bill on how to help the Social Security/homeless/dying/sick/poor/handicapped/ethnic/elderly/minority/disenfranchised/unemployed/homely/uneducated/short/pregnant/almost pregnant/want to be pregnant/hate to be pregnant pathetic forgotten lost souls."

Geraldine Ferraro had a party, Caroline Kennedy made a speech, Gloria Steinem hosted a fund-raiser, Norman Mailer was BSing with everybody, Jackie O.'s one-time live-in Maurice Tempelsman was running around with a patriotic ribbon around his neck. Chastity Bono, who was speaking for the gay community, arrived with a girlfriend. The music was so loud we couldn't talk. When I could read her lips she was saying, "I gave up my band for a career in politics."

All this was going on in between my phoning my sweetie. I hated that he was away from me. I wanted him to hear my voice. I knew if he did he'd rush over, lick the phone, and bark. This would constitute a successful communication between us and I wouldn't feel so guilty. Or so lonely.

At political conventions everyone's fighting for something. This one wants to change abortion rights. This one wants a change in welfare. This one wants a change in government. Me, I wanted a change in underwear. My panties were getting tight. I don't say those in the business of public service are hefty. Let's put it this way, wherever they stood the plants died. Nothing grows in the shade. Whether they were voting for a platform that puts rear ends front and center or fighting to put hindquarters on the table, I'm not sure. I'm only sure "it" was happening to me, too.

The reason every committee woman was shaped like Danny DeVito became clear to me. Food. The lack of portion control and the quantity of junk available. Out of nervousness I, too, was inhaling pails of cardboard food. Chips, dips, sips. Off paper plates so thin that the mayonnaise in the tuna salad leaked through. Accompanied by plastic cups so small a sparrow could die of thirst.

By day four, I'd puffed out so much I could fit into only Fruit of the Looms and the two "fat" dresses I'd saved from years ago. My best "in case" fat dress was a short-sleeved, hot pink suede designer dress with bone suede collar and bone suede cuffs. It had cost a fortune but, back when I was chunky, price was no object. The real object being, despite my suet-logged bones I had to look good.

I was lonely. Also miserable. I was tired from working

nonstop, but I missed my dog. I decided I couldn't survive if I didn't make the five-hour round-trip drive the next day just to see his sweet face and pet him for a half hour. Maybe this dog could make it without me, but I couldn't make it without him. I therefore put on the hot pink suede designer dress so I could drive right down to work next morning early, without changing clothes.

It had been raining. A big rain. The ground underneath us was muddy. To prevent Jazzy from triple somersaulting into my arms when he saw me, his handlers set him down carefully on a dry section of the road. I bent down to coochie-coo him. In his excitement he splashed right into a puddle, then hurled himself straight onto my bosom.

All four paws are forever imprinted on that chest. Not even the *Enola Gay* could wipe off those stains. My short-sleeved hot pink suede designer dress now had a permanent dalmatian print.

I had to stop by the apartment and quick-change into the Albert Nippon two-piece red-and-white polka-dot cotton I'd bought at the height of chunkiness five years earlier. I kept it for just such emergencies. Nothing so great you'd be knighted in it, but not a shame for the neighbors. It did the job when you couldn't button anything else.

So, cloaking my lumpy bones in this number, I sallied forth to meet and greet. One of the first people I bumped into was Maryland's lieutenant governor, Kathleen Kennedy Townsend, daughter of Ethel and Robert Kennedy.

This public figure steeped in diplomacy and the political art of saying nothing spurts out, "My God, you're still wearing *that?* I had it years ago. I've already thrown it out."

I stared at her in horror. The lieutenant governor, whose smarts were obviously such that I couldn't see how she could ever make governor, realized her mistake instantly. Even as it was tumbling out she sort of burbled an apology. Too late. My feelings, my aura, my friends, my dress—all wilted.

In this dismal frame I returned to my only true love. The one constant. The lone creature alive who loved me unconditionally—no matter how fat, how tacky, how old my wardrobe.

I myself drove another two and a half hours to pick him up. In my excitement I raced up to the meadow where he was playing. I shouted: "Jazzy . . . baby . . . it's me, Mommy . . . Come to me . . ."

Those two pointy ears, which you cautioned to shave in a V-form so the weight of the growing hairs don't pull them down, twisted and turned in an aerial-like manner. They saw me. They heard me. They caught me. They made me. And Jazzy responded immediately—by running in the opposite direction. I don't mean he grazed there on his way. I mean he set his tail ESE, toward my face, and raced away from me full steam.

Hidden in the tall grass, I could barely make out the tips of those ears. He wouldn't come to me. Eventually we collared him, got him in the car, and drove him home. He wasn't having any of it. He wouldn't come for food, wouldn't approach for the usual garden-variety hugging. I offered a lamb chop, which he'd usually kill for.

Nothing.

Jazzy was having major attitude. Annoyed that I'd left him. He wasn't going to give me an inch no matter how long I lay on the ground. My tiny Yorkshire terrier lite, who couldn't eat unless I fed him, couldn't drink unless I gave him water, couldn't find shelter unless I provided it, couldn't get clean unless I bathed him, couldn't get healthy unless I took him to the vet, was going to teach me a lesson.

I cradled him like a lover. I scratched his belly like he always loved me to do. I rubbed him under the neck like he always loved me to do. I went out and got him a bone from Gallagher's steakhouse.

Nothing.

It took three days before he'd even talk to me. It's a

record of some sort. In one week, dissed by Maryland's lieutenant governor and dissed by my in-house prince.

Meanwhile, I had business to conduct with real royalty. I had an interview one evening with Her Semi-Royal Highness Sarah Ferguson, duchess of York, ex-daughter-in-law of Elizabeth the queen, former wife of Prince Andrew, second son of Her Majesty, brother of we-should-live-so-long, the future king of England.

This meant I must leave Prince Jazzy at home alone. This was not a welcome prospect. Jazzy does not like to be home alone. I tried bribing him. I played mind games with him. I prepared a bowl of food, freshly warmed, just the way he likes it, poured him a bowl of Poland Spring water, laid out his favorite chew toys, opened the window a room away just a fraction so there'd be proper air, turned on the lights, put on the TV to the Cartoon Network, set the thermostat at a cozy 75, and placed my boy in his custom-made doggy bed—the one with his face carved on the headboard—and tucked in his personal blanket—the one with his name embroidered on it. I sallied forth at 5 P.M.

The royal visit was just us. The used-to-be duchess and the want-to-be diva. Fergie had rung me from England and we'd arranged to have this date. We shared mayonnaisey-runny egg sandwiches that dribbled with every bite. Her Royal Highness, being classier than myself, spooned the glop off the carpet of her suite at the Hotel Carlyle. Me, I licked mine off my fingers.

We gossiped. I asked what's the queen drag around in those big clunky handbags of hers since we know she doesn't carry any money, bus tokens, or keys to the kingdom. The answer was a hanky and makeup.

Fergie said Her Majesty actually "has a sense of humor. The queen appears austere but really loves to laugh."

Since I somehow don't see Elizabeth, ruler of England, Scotland, Wales, part of Ireland, and none of her children, on *Saturday Night Live,* the subject switched to Fergie's superskinniness and how she initially lost those first fourteen pounds.

"I had just plain gotten fat and I just plain had to lose weight," she told me. "So what I did was, I ate chicken salad for lunch and chicken salad for dinner for weeks. Breakfast was a boiled egg and grapefruit."

She sported a knockout ruby ring plus a heart-shaped diamond ring and black lizard pumps and black-and-white designer suit and looked nifty.

"I have a fat wardrobe and a thin wardrobe," she sighed. "I even take it out on my children. Because of me they have to diet, too. When Lent came one child gave up her favorite tomato ketchup. This lasted three days. The other gave up sweets. That lasted an hour."

Flowers arrived for HRH. Then T-shirts from some company arrived. Then she spooned up the cakes that had come on our tray. "Comfort food," she said. "I'm just in need of some comfort food."

"Right," I said, vacuuming up whatever she didn't finish.

"I guess Lent is what really helped me. I had to give up my favorite white wine for Lent. That was hard."

So if it was hard, how did she do it?

Grinned the duchess of York, "I switched to red."

A couple of hours later I walked home in a euphoric state. I'd knocked off this exclusive juicy sit-down with royalty. I was pretty proud of myself.

My dog was not impressed.

When I arrived home I'd considered it the perfect segue. Brit to Brit. Duchess of York to terrier from York.

Uh-uh.

My roommate was in a royal snit. The queen's an amateur in comparison. Jazzy not only hadn't eaten, he had tracked his yummies around the room.

My guilt was complete. I had abandoned my darling and now he was refusing to eat. So, fresh from my royal encounter, I lay flat on the floor, my white coat smack across the tiles. I gurgled and *goo-goo*ed this beauty of mine. I hand-fed him a fresh, home-cooked serving of skinless boiled chicken and rice. Me, I'd wolfed down one lone cold crustless sandwich. Jazzy I'd made a whole hot meal.

I sang, I hummed. On the floor I did a handicapped version of the rumba, I *good-boy*ed him, I waved the spoon up and down and in and out, and he turned his behind to me and waddled away.

Ignoring me, he yawned and sprawled out on one of the overstuffed armchairs. He then wriggled himself sideways to watch Mommy make a fool of herself. Not knowing quite what to do, I took a spoonful of his dinner from the bowl and walked this one spoonful across the whole room to where he lay in state. He honored me by nibbling. Just the bits of chicken and steak. He plucked them out of the mixed-in rice and dry Eukaneuba. The rice and Eukaneuba now dropped to the floor. I didn't have a whole lot of choice, so I picked it up. Sweet Jazzy with his angelic face lay there watching me, as though to say, "I'll teach you for leaving me flat."

What to do? I now brought his whole bowl over. He

ignored it and me again. I returned the damn bowl to its usual position, and again shoveled up another spoonful to walk it all the way across the room. He picked out the bits of chicken and steak and dribbled the rice and Eukaneuba on the floor.

And then fixed me with a look that's Castilian Yorkie for, "Up yours."

Something was wrong with the way I lived. Earlier I'd soared on the wings of angels, rubbing shoulders with such a demanding divinity as a *genyoowine* international personality. Now I was flat on the floor, prostrating my belly before such a dogged diva as a Yorkshire terrier.

From the Duchess of York to the terrier from York.

Fergie was easier.

CHAPTER 15

Shoe Business

Come Labor Day there is absolutely no other place in the world to be than New York. There are even songs about autumn in New York. Store windows are dazzling, people are bustling, industry is flourishing. It's executives in suits and ties brown-bagging it on stone steps, Rollerbladers on the sidewalk, bicyclists on the street, ice cream trucks on the corner, lovers riding hansom cabs on Fifth Avenue.

It's artists in Central Park bargaining with tourists. Kids selling colored cotton candy on the sidewalk. Hustlers peddling warm Prada handbags off a blanket right outside Bloomingdale's. New Yorkers on the go eating franks, pretzels, frozen yogurt, pizzas, hamburgers, nuts, fruits, salads in plastic containers, candy, cookies, bagels.

In the park it's magicians, jugglers, a sea of bodies on benches catching the sun's last rays, tourists in hot pink and bright orange carrying cameras and maps, street performers tootling saxophones.

And runners. In New York nobody strolls in a leisurely fashion. You're either a jogger trying to keep your figure or a pedestrian trying to keep your wallet. But everybody runs. And with our wall-to-wall gridlock (despite signs that say no standing, no stopping, no parking, no kidding), it's faster, too. A survey has determined that the only way to alleviate Manhattan's traffic problem is to legalize car theft.

And every-single-body is hauling a bottle of water. In days of yore, who knew from lugging water bags, canteens, flasks, or thermoses? Today, forget about an American Express card. What humans wouldn't think of leaving home without is a water jug.

In autumn the world is out promenading. Such as the fat fat man with the profile like a set of keys. The stomach jutting out like a peninsula, then hanging over his belt pancake-style. Such as youngsters holding hands. Trying to determine if they're in love. They'll soon learn the only fail-safe test is to ask themselves, "Would I mind being financially destroyed by this person?" Such as the woman who sports skirts to the ankle in summer and, with cool weather approaching, wears minis so mini the hemline barely clears her navel. And dark glasses. Even on dim, rainy days, dark glasses.

Autumn in New York. I felt, once again, glad to be alive. Grateful for my friends, for my work, for the activity around me. Jolie Gabor (mother of Zsa Zsa), in her hundredth year, had told me, "Dollingk, for a lady alone there is no place to live but New York. New York is life."

Of all the tender shoots taking root in this, my second life, the one grabbing hold the most was that teeny being. That being who isn't even as high as my teased hair. Jazzy had become an addiction. As absolutely addicting as nicotine or pot or booze or carbs.

He's slightly bowlegged. In the rear he's all silver blue except for one shock right around his tail. That's beige. His tiny face is so picture-perfect you just want to hold it and love it and kiss it.

With the weather so perfect I took Jazzy along on my errands. I took him wherever I could.

We'd spent months training him. Teaching him to walk with me just like a proper gentleman. To promenade directly alongside me, stay in step with me, keep my pace, remain always on my left side, respond to the word "heel." In extremis I could slap my thigh lightly, yank slightly on the leash, and raise my voice when I uttered the magic word "heel," but he was obeying so well that this seemed no longer necessary.

I was proud of him. He'd come a long way.

Thus, one glorious afternoon, I took him shopping on Fifth Avenue. Head high, credit card akimbo, Madam and mutt minced into Gucci. As we crossed the threshold, the doorman, whose nose was up so high that if he sneezed he'd blow his brains out, said, "Madam, you forgot something."

He pointed. I looked. My dog, moving with the grace and perfection of a Nureyev, had blown the rest of his manners. Without missing a beat he'd dropped a package at the doorman's boot. It was tapping as the doorman stood in place watching me scurry about for a plastic bag.

Such are the humiliations visited upon us by our family members. Now I knew how the late Milton Berle's kin felt when he did a radio show a while back and waxed rhapsodic about how God was good to him and granted him long life, enough to enjoy his two delicious grandchildren, Anthony and Deirdre. He then came home. In a larynx coated with ice his wife announced, "Milton, those are *not* your grandchildren's names."

Altogether, this first day shopping with Jazzy was not a winner. Hustling out of Gucci, it was on to Saks Fifth.

Mac Cosmetics was having a promotion at their counter. My dog created a commotion. A manager brought him water. In the excitement he upended the water and we were sliding. His leash became entangled with shoppers' feet. A salesgirl unhooked it so he didn't strangle himself. I panicked and said, "He needs his leash. There's too much confusion here." A European lady in a long A-line coat swiftly tucked him underneath so he wouldn't be stepped on and he was hidden and I couldn't find him. When I finally wrenched him away from inside that Good Samaritan's lining, I folded him under my arm and ran out.

Jazzy's first shopping trip was less than elegant. But he informed me he wasn't about to be a homebody. He was a dog on the town.

My driver, Reggie, has been with me twenty-four years. He's part of my extended family and I treasure him. Reggie is tall and weighs a good two hundred pounds. His friend Doug runs a garage. Doug is major-size. Way over six feet and, maybe, three hundred pounds. One day when we were out for a drive, Reggie pulled into Doug's garage to check the brake fluid. I hopped out and went to retrieve something from the trunk while Reggie called Doug over.

Doug's garage has housed John Fitzgerald Kennedy's

green BMW and taken care of wheels belonging to Rush Limbaugh and the assorted limos of Mariah Carey. Doug is not exactly the type to be blown away by Jazzy Adams, Esq.—especially since Doug figured correctly that Jazzy was not a tipper.

Doug looked straight down and said, "Reggie, what is *that*?"

"That," said Reggie, "is a genuine pedigreed champion Yorkie. It's Mrs. Adams's dog."

"Hey," said Doug, wielding a broom, "I got no time for this. I have to clean the garage."

"Man," said Reggie, ruffling Jazzy's ear with one finger, "watch your mouth. This little boy steals your heart. Everyplace we go people faint for this dog. I'm crazy for this dog. I love this dog. You just got to love Jazzy."

"Man," said Doug, "you are going either soft or gay or nuts."

"Trust me, Doug, you don't know what you're talking about," said Reggie, who by then was trying to extricate Doug's broom from Jazzy's jaws.

Reggie excused himself to go to the john and returned to find Big Doug hopelessly involved in pitting his huge size and muscle in a game of fetch with a Yorkie who was smaller than his hand.

We are not talking Akita, malamute, dalmatian,

Doberman, rottweiler, or husky. The point is, once you start with these toy breeds that you can carry in your sleeve, you can't stop. The first time you make that initial contact, the first time you make that itty-bitty baby talk like, "C'mere, you little poo-poo," the first time that scraggly little fluff ball wags its teeny tail and those ears stand up, you are gone.

Gone was Doug's parking the cars or swabbing the windshields. Doug was in the coochie-cooing mode: "Ohhhh, is he cute . . . ohhhh, so adorable . . . Ohh, Jazzy sweetie booby boobly bubby beeby bibby baby . . ."

That he could grab your heart, there was no doubt. That he was a wicked terror, also no doubt. Jazzy's major pleasure was eating shoes. Sneakers he didn't care a lot for. Skin shoes he liked. My black lizards went soon after he arrived. Next came the spike heels of my black-and-white snakeskins. Gnawed right through to the wood, they were. I flopped right down on all fours and eyeball-to-eyeball told Jazzy right to his face, "Do that one more time and I'm going to sew you right onto my winter hat."

I couldn't return the shoes. All I could do was chalk it up to the cost of owning this beloved, worshipped Yorkshire terrier of mine.

I was told he does this because he's bored. Hey, I also get bored occasionally, but it doesn't mean I can eat my neighbor's slingbacks. He needs chew toys, they told me. This lightweight already had more chew toys than Monica Lewinsky. I was basically handling the situation— until the Houseguest.

Lana Marks was my houseguest. A South African whose home is now Palm Beach, she's possibly today's numero uno alligator handbag maker. She has shops everywhere. Her Madison Avenue boutique is two blocks from my apartment. Lana's bags have been featured in so many movies she should win an Oscar. In the film *Autumn in New York*, Winona Ryder swipes Richard Gere with her L.M. purse. Filming *Beautiful Joe*, Sharon Stone's mislaid fake braids were found inside her lime green L.M. tote. In *Unconditional Love*'s funeral scene, Lynn Redgrave, Kathy Bates, and Julie Andrews all carry you-know-whats. In *Ms. Congeniality*, Sandra Bullock carries a lavender L.M. clutch. In *Novocaine*, Laura Dern schleps a black carryall with tortoise trim, made by Lana. In *The Tailor of Panama*, Jamie Lee Curtis sports Lana's ostrich number.

It was coming up on Fashion Week, one of the big fall events in New York, and Lana was staying at my apartment for two days. She arrived carrying a drop-dead-gorgeous lilac alligator bag. The matching lilac alligator high-heeled pumps, she'd paid $2,500 for. Understand, not everyone has lilac alligator shoes. In fact, most folks don't even have black alligator shoes. When Lana finally kicked off those shoes and flopped down in my guest room, it was the end of a hard day. Organizing a layout for *Vogue,* meeting with shoppers for *Oprah.*

We were going to dinner later, but I had to race out for a quickie in-person interview with Peter Fonda. Peter was in town hustling a movie in which he was then starring. He was sandwiching in TV interviews and had about twenty free minutes between a fast massage and another show. We were to meet directly across the street, so I definitely wasn't going to be away longer than a half hour.

I don't know what triggered Peter's train of thought but, sitting at the Four Seasons Hotel, he was opining politically. So I just wound him up and let him go.

"I'd make a good president," he said. "I'd be honest. I already know all about the bad stuff you shouldn't do because I've been there. I don't want to be president, but I would if there were such extraordinary emergencies that our already bad infrastructure totally breaks down. In that case I'd not hesitate to declare martial law. I'd call on every governor to call out their National Guard."

Okay.

"I'd get rid of the whole government, then replace both houses so life continues since mail has to be delivered, food must be disseminated. I'd disallow anyone to rerun for office, limit all political campaigns to five thousand dollars, and all public service to two terms."

Okay.

"I'd fire every federal judge because they're the most corrupt of the bunch. I'd keep in place only the Supreme Court. I'd lock them into their building. They'd slip papers out to me, I'd slip meals into them—until they could put democracy in place."

Okay.

"And once I'd readied the new infrastructure and seen that we all returned to the Bill of Rights, I'd go back to my ranch in Montana and hope I get another movie."

Right. Now that I'd just taken Fractured Politics 101, I wanted to get home to my houseguest.

Lana Marks usually stayed at the Plaza Hotel, which you can see from my window. It certainly had better room service than I was willing to provide, and I asked why she preferred being a houseguest to a hotel guest. She said, "I do so much traveling. My husband doesn't come along and so I'm always out there on my own. It's nice to have someone to come back to."

I, thus, was eager to hurry back. I rushed in and was not greeted by the usual barking and yipping. There was Lana Marks, designer to the rich and fabulous, relaxing.

Head back, eyes closed, shoes off. Or, that is, head back, eyes closed, shoes gone.

There was Jazzy. Serene. In ecstasy. Rolling around in strips of alligator. He had eaten his way through to the canvas of one lilac alligator pump and was getting ready to start on the second.

It was the Houseguest's only pair of shoes since she was flying home the next evening. In any case, it was for sure her only pair of lilac alligator shoes to match her purse and her suit, and she had a full day coming up with the fashion press.

What could I do? What could I say? I looked at the Houseguest and her elevated stocking'd feet and I said only, "There's no business like shoe business."

CHAPTER 16

Sibling Rivalry

We'd become a bona fide, official couple. It used to be people would ask, "How are you?" and I'd say, "Fine," and then they'd ask, "And how's Joey?" and I'd say, "He's fine." Now it was, "How are you?" "Fine." "And how's Jazzy?" "Fine." It was Jazzy and Cindy. The couple of the moment. In olden days invitations came to the house addressed, "Cindy and Joey Adams." Now they came addressed, "Cindy and Jazzy Adams."

Suddenly, I was inundated with doggy dreck. Birthday, Mother's Day, whatever day—I'd receive doggy cakes, doggy cookies, photos of canines, toys (although my crea-

ture still preferred to play with an old toothbrush and a
ballpoint pen), doggy fragrances, shampoos, leashes,
bowls, necklaces, beads, beds, bows. I was living and
breathing dog.

Never having had children, it was becoming clear that
I wasn't a good mommy type. I not only gave my son too
much, I was overly nervous. I hovered. I fretted. Wouldn't
let him in the park for fear he'd eat dirt. Wouldn't allow
him on our terrace alone lest he chew a toxic leaf. The terror that something might happen to this love of my life
was tormenting. That's when I decided Jazzy could no
longer be an only dog. He had to have a brother or sister.

I'd recently been to the Bahamas. In 1994, Sol
Kerzner, born in South Africa to Russian Jewish immi-
grants, bought Merv Griffin's Paradise Island property.
Some $850 million later it became Atlantis, a 1,174-room
hotel and casino. Michael Jordan stays in its $25,000-a-
night Bridge Suite. Michael Jackson is a steady visitor.
Ditto Julia Roberts. Elton John works for Sol, Leonardo
DiCaprio takes invitations from him, Cindy Crawford
got married at his place, Prince Philip favors him, and the
day I rang a voice in the background shouted, "Sharon
Stone on line one!"

It's where Gloria Estefan's Latin album *Caribbean Soul*
premiered, where I personally saw King World's Roger

King at a five hundred-dollar blackjack table with a hundred grand stacked in front of him, and where they made a first-time exemption for Oprah in that she was permitted to room with her dog.

My flight down carried Diane Von Furstenburg, whose mom lived nearby. At my first dinner I met Nora McCaniff, president of *People* magazine, whose conversation turned to Yorkie Rescue—a nonprofit national operation that rescues Yorkies and places them in loving homes.

I thought to myself, "Aha! Of course. That's it! God's way of telling me this is what I should do. I will rescue and adopt a lost, unclaimed, unwanted Yorkie. I will become heroic. I will become knighted. I shall become henceforth and therewith heretofore known as St. Cindy, patroness of terriers. Or terrible patroness. Or something."

So I said to my PR friend Geoffrey Weill, "I want another dog."

He was baffled. "What do you mean, you want another dog?"

"Am I not speaking English? Repeat after me—*dog*. A three-letter word meaning human's best friend. Woof woof. Bowwow."

"How can you handle another dog when you can't handle the one you've got?" he asked logically.

I sighed heavily. "Please, I want to give an unwanted, abused animal a home."

Looking at me the way George Burns used to look at Gracie Allen, Geoffrey said, "Dear, you cannot give another dog a home—because the home you live in your existing dog already owns."

"Please," I said. "The real problem is I am agonizing over bringing competition into the house. Will Jazzy accept it? Should it be a boy or a girl? Younger or older? Smaller or larger? Long hair? Short hair? Tamer? Gentler? Cat?"

"How about a reptile."

"Definitely no. An iguana would clash with my drapes."

"Goldfish?"

"Can't pet them."

"Gerbils?"

"Not my style. Mice I don't dig. And other than stuffing them with bread and chestnuts, I don't know what to do with birds."

"You don't know what to do with dogs, either. You've reared a four-legged king."

"All I'm doing is loving him. And what you don't understand is, I don't want Jazzy to be an only dog."

THE GIFT OF Jazzy

"Listen, there is no daddy in this house. He's left his brothers and sisters to come and live here with you. He is not an only dog. What he is, is a single-parent dog."

Geoffrey then looked right into my eyes. "Jazzy is never going to share you. Forget it."

Convinced this longtime dog lover didn't know what he was talking about, I phoned Ellen, the superperson who, despite her own career, works almost ceaselessly and for nothing, just for the love of these homeless Yorkies.

I said, "I don't know quite how to do this."

"Don't worry. We do this all the time," Ellen said. "We'll show you."

"Do you have anyone available at the moment?"

"I have a beautiful girl dog whom we rescued on the streets of Philadelphia. She's coming in this week."

"What's she doing in Philadelphia?"

"We don't know exactly. But she was found off her leash and nobody's claimed her. Our people have the feeling her parents took off for other places and couldn't take her along. That sometimes happens, you know. They get a job in another city and can't take a pet or the new home won't accept them or their owner's getting a divorce and the new relationship is allergic or doesn't want a dog. So what they do is they just let them loose."

I couldn't bear it. "I'll take her," I said. "Is she healthy? Is she all right? I wouldn't want to infect Jazzy."

"The reason we won't bring her in until later this week is that we're checking her out with the vet. She's getting her shots. She's clean and she's about six months old."

Then I worried about her disposition. "What about temperament? Your dog won't eat my dog, will she? I think I need a pleasant, docile type."

"She's a very sweet, gentle animal."

"Neutered? I'm not ready to be a mother-in-law."

"Yes. Neutered. She's a bit wobbly, though. Like she's been scared or something. Her little legs are weak. That's the only problem."

I was so busy. I bought new bowls for her, new toys, new doggy beds. In advance of her coming I rang dog psychologists to inquire how I should introduce the new arrival to the resident Top Dog. I asked what I must do to make sure Jazzy didn't treat the new arrival like an hors d'oeuvre.

I was told to introduce them on neutral territory, then take Jazzy home alone. Reintroduce them again on neutral turf. Let them check each other out. After a few such play sessions I should begin putting them together. "Don't

rush," said one. "Think how you'd feel if suddenly someone moved into your home. It becomes crowded, it's a
fight for space, schedules change, foods reflect others'
tastes, privacy isn't what it used to be. It's no different
with a Fido and a Fluffy."

Other owners advised that I begin having serious dia-
logues with Jazzy. Prepare him.

So I sat on the floor and began a conversation. And I
told Jazzy, "Dog," I said, "you are about to have a sister."

He cocked his head to the side. I had the uncomfort-
able feeling that he was thinking, "Living with a gossip
columnist is tough. She wags her tongue more than I wag
my tail."

"I don't want you to be lonely or grow up spoiled," I
said.

Jazzy fixed me with that hangdog expression that
probably said, "I knew when I came here that this woman
would need a lot of training."

He was looking at me. I noticed he wasn't smiling.
Then I realized I'd never seen him smile. Maybe dogs do
not ever smile. That set me to thinking he should smile.
Like what the hell has he got to be cranky about? If he's
living a dog's life, it's a pretty good one.

Later that week Bailey from the Yorkie rescue service

arrived. So scared. And such a delicious, darling, dear face. I made the mistake of taking her sweet face in my two hands and kissing it.

Jazzy turned into Simba, king of the jungle. The low growl came from deep within his gizzard. His tail did not wag and he began a never-ending cacophony of short barks. Little Bailey, who was even smaller than Jazzy, was frozen in terror.

She was unfamiliar with the surroundings, she didn't know where and what, everything was strange, she'd lost her mother and father and home, who knows what had befallen her and for how long on the streets. She was terrified. And for sure she wasn't being welcomed by her new half brother.

I didn't know what I was supposed to do. I thought if I just loved her, how wrong could that be? So I picked her up and stroked her.

Wrong move. Jazzy lunged for her. When, eventually, I had to set her down he body-slammed her.

She walked away from him. I thought the answer is food. I must feed this poor child. I set food down in her bowl. Jazzy went for it. I hollered at Jazzy. It made him even wilder. He circled her. I picked him up to try and break the jealous cycle and cuddled him. He wriggled out of my arms and began hassling her.

"It's what I call the Charles Bronson bully syndrome," said Warren Eckstine. "Jazzy's the type who, if he could, would have a tattoo and be wearing a black leather jacket. You're going to have to negotiate with him."

And then I realized this dear little Bailey was not well. She wobbled badly. She could barely walk. She slid. Ellen had brought me pills to give her three times a day. She told me that Bailey had been ailing when they found her and that she was now 80 percent okay and getting stronger every day. But whether from nerves or fear or the residual effects of having been ill, Bailey couldn't hold her water. Or anything else. She was losing it all over my floor.

I loved this gentle, frightened puppy whose eyes were fearful and who trembled in my arms. I stayed up all night comforting her. I faithfully fed her the medication. I gave her toys to play with, but Jazzy took them away. I put her in another room, but it didn't work because I kept running back and forth all weekend to tend to the one, then to the other. I became a nervous wreck.

I didn't sleep. I couldn't sleep. And my main goal—to please Jazzy—was totally lost. He was seriously unhappy. He was bent on destroying Bailey. So I wasn't pleasing Jazzy and I wasn't helping Bailey and I was knocking myself out.

Bailey clearly was going to have her healing deterred by the presence of an aggressive, possessive Jazzy. Bailey needed to be in a home where there was no controversy, no jealousy, only someone to love her and care for her. She needed quiet and she needed nursing and she needed undivided attention.

I was devastated that I had to give her back. Ellen came and took her, and I kept in touch until I knew she'd been given a proper home. Ellen finally placed her with a senior citizen lady who lived alone and could give her all the peace and nurturing she needed.

I shed a tear and then said a prayer for Ellen and for Bailey and for the woman who has since been protecting her. And for Jazzy? I decided I had to give him a party for his first birthday. Only celebrity dogs. As befitting his station. I mean, naturally.

I realized I was going to the dogs. I realized I was not being true to my husband's memory. I realized that it was too early for me to be in love. But what can I tell you? I was sharing my bed with another male, and this newest love of my life was having a birthday. On September 29 he was a year old.

Each year of our lives together I had given a party for Joey's birthday. I well recall what I went through for his final gala. When Joey saw the guest list, which ran from Imelda Marcos to Leona Helmsley, he cracked, "If you're indicted you're invited." But it wasn't the celebrities who stick in my mind, it was the wardrobe. He'd gotten schloompy in his latter days.

A month before the Big Night he had complained, "I can't fit into my tuxedos."

"You can't fit into your nontuxedos, either."

The last time I had stuffed him into a tux I'd had to promise sex and guarantee my mother wouldn't phone for a week. I now figured none of those hardships were worth it.

"I'll wear a turtleneck," he said. "It's cold outside."

"Yes, but the party's inside."

And then there was the matter of his fur boots. He'd developed a love for fleece-lined ankle boots. He'd even worn a pair to a July garden party.

"They're soft. They make my bunion feel good."

"Right. But why make a bunion comfortable? Why not have a podiatrist remove the bunion?"

"They're roomy without falling off my feet. Good for walking."

"What walking? You use your car to go from the bed to the john. Walk where? Certainly not to your shirt maker."

And there was his antique John Weitz pile-lined raincoat. Centuries ago he'd lost the belt, although the loops remained. One buckle at the wrist had broken so the thing was lopsided. A pocket was slightly torn thanks to the pennies he was collecting for our elevator man's baby son. I'd say this coat had given Joey his money's worth except he hadn't paid for it in the first place. John had given it to him as a gift.

Alan Alda, Tony Bennett, Regis Philbin, George Steinbrenner, the mayor, the governor, the cardinal, the whole city was getting set for Joey's party. The only one who couldn't get himself set was Joey. He needed a clothing specialist. He wanted a second opinion.

"My favorite single-breasted is still good."

"If you don't mind a belt in the back and four buttons. You look like an umpire."

"What are you talking about? Black mohair is very in."

"Yes. But when you first bought that suit it was gray worsted."

"You saying it's shiny?"

"I'm saying that if you fell down you'd get seven years' bad luck."

"Please. It's conservative. I like conservative."

"Conservative is one thing. Retarded is another."

Joey was very into this one suit, although the hem of the left cuff dragged and loose threads dangled from the jacket lining. He sported it to weddings and he wore it to the incinerator. He never took it off. To get it cleaned we had to give him gas.

The day of the party I saw that black mohair still hanging front and center in the closet next to the brand-new navy blue two-vent job I'd had made for him. I was so frightened that I took a pair of scissors and cut off the mohair's right leg at the knee.

His screams were heard all the way to the ballroom.

So now it was time for the birthday party for the new male in my life. What an occasion it was going to be.

Peter Max wanted to borrow a dog so that he could come. I told him no. Not fair. Barbara Taylor Bradford wanted to bring both her dogs. I told her no. One per VIP. Bobby Short has a dalmatian named Chili. I had to say no to him, too. Only small dogs. Lapdogs. Toy dogs. I wasn't a kennel.

There was Dick Cavett, Catherine Hickland of *One Life to Live,* Erica Jong, Oleg Cassini leading Rambo.

Arlene Dahl's schnauzer Hansel sported a red rhinestone collar. Bryant Gumble with his white fluffy Maltese Cujo. Mary Tyler Moore's schnauzer was Shayna, as in "shayna maidel," which means "pretty girl" in Yiddish. Sally Jessy Raphael came with her affenpinscher Lisa. Chazz Palminteri escorted his wife Gina and son Dante and some hound that I can't remember. Red-haired socialite Georgette Mosbacher, major fund-raiser for the GOP, had Eve, a cavalier King Charles spaniel with hair as red as hers. Danny Aiello had to beg off. He's dogless. Allergic. Celeste Holm was teary. She'd just lost hers. Chris Lawford's, Carol Ladd's, and Cheryl Tiegs's hounds were in California.

What started as a cute and fun idea became a doggone big deal. My building wanted a liability policy. My own people made me take a similar umbrella.

I had ten handlers. To differentiate them from the other two-footed guests, I had aprons embroidered with the name *Jazzy*.

We had custom-made doggy bags. We had sterling silver collars made for them. A special john, behind doggy gates, was readied for those who were antisocial. Owners were told to walk their ferocious killer beasts beforehand. This way, when time came for them to leave and go back to their homes, I'd still have a home to go back to, too.

All this for a five-pound hair ball. If I'd put this much effort into a two-hundred-pound lover, at least there would be some perks. He could do the dishes.

CHAPTER 17

Jazzy's Phone Fetish

There are short periods when Jazzy and I are a Norman Rockwell painting. Me in a rocking chair, shod in woolly slippers, and my best friend benignly at my feet. We can be Krazy-Glued together for an hour straight and he can snooze peacefully without exchanging one bark with me, his head burrowing quietly in his bed, never even turning in my direction. That is, until the telephone rings.

That one single sound triggers some maniacal, crazed angst.

Unfortunately for my darling pup's equilibrium, the telephone is a big number in our house.

For me an office at home is necessary because, as a journalist who writes a column six days a week, notes and files are needed at all hours. I'm the front line for everyone's misfortune. Someone's been indicted, someone's in a train wreck, someone's ill, someone's kid is on a drug trip. Our City Desk has a knee-jerk reaction to big-name tragedies that occur late at night: Wake up Cindy.

It has always been thus. Take my virgin experience with a *Post* obit. They rang me at midnight to announce that Grace Kelly had just died. Before I could suck in my breath, the clipped voice on the other end said, "We need twenty inches. You got ten minutes."

It took me those ten minutes to get over the triple shock. One, that Princess Grace of Monaco was dead in a freak accident. Two, that the voice on the other end of the phone had been totally without emotion. It was business as usual. And three, that I actually had to get a 750-word appreciation piece together in two more minutes.

With the time difference, Europeans ring you at the crack of dawn. Californians return calls after lunchtime, which is your early evening. Those in the Far East dial in the middle of your night.

I have five telephone lines. Two incoming, three outgoing. Incoming are red, outgoing black. Plus fax lines, plus modem lines. There's no turning this world off.

When I'm getting dressed, the phone rings. I'm getting a home manicure, my ten fingers stuck straight up in the air like a scrub nurse in an operating room, the phone rings. One day a doctor is going to be summoned to surgically remove a phone from my ear.

It was becoming apparent that I had to upgrade my equipment. In Joey's waning years he no longer went to his office. He was home all the time. Our telephone equipment had to be as simple and free of bells and whistles as possible so that he could use it. Now that he was gone I wanted to join the twenty-first century in terms of technology. Also I'd suffered with interference on the line for a year. So in came the phone company, which started life as AT&T, then became NY Telephone, then got married for a few minutes to something called Lucent, which spawned the baby Bell Atlantic, which is now Verizon. Eventually, whatever these people are called this season, they came to my apartment and installed a state-of-the-art communications system. The White House didn't have such sophisticated stuff.

The panel board looked like a 747 cockpit. This is call waiting, this is call forwarding. This is redial. This is conference. This is automatic dial. This is fax. This is second fax. This is intercom. This is answering machine. This is caller ID. This is so you talk hands-free. This is to patch into your office downtown. This is to connect to another part of the house. This is to store the last number called. This is to cancel the last number called. This is memory, to hold on to the last number you called. This is to punch up the photo of the caller. This is to lower the ring. This is to raise the ring. This is to reach your car. This is to reach your editor. This is to tell the time. This is to fix the time. This is to tell the date. This to correct the date. This is Press One for voice mail. Press Two to cancel Press One. Press Three to reinstate Press One.

It was spectacular—except for one thing. When the phone rang I didn't know what to push. I needed to enroll in night school just to understand my phone system. I would have preferred a rotary dial. Anything. Just so I could answer a jangling telephone.

One evening I was so frustrated that I ripped out the cord and went back to my simple basic instrument. I just plugged the old jack right into the wall, and voilà! I could make a phone call. Of course, when this antique plain vanilla phone came back the interference on the line also came back. This time I figured out what it was. My dog.

Jazzy had by now realized that when my hand touched that bone-shaped instrument, I somehow ended up making sounds into it. He also figured out that when I was talking to it, I was not all that interested in talking to him. Jazzy does not know from time-sharing. He shares nothing—not toys, not attention. The dog should have been named Donald Trump.

He therefore was not passive about the phone. It took away from him. He is a certified selfish dog. The noise of a phone ringing is the same to him as the sound of buckshot to a deer. Makes him take off like a bat out of hell. He'll leap over furniture, vault sofas, ford a stream, charge across a crowded room, ignore a special dessert delight like a rawhide bone stuffed with Kraft, to get to it before anyone else. He'll knock it over. He'll bark into it. The perfect pet for a gossip columnist. Jazzy, too, is into gossip.

Gossip is as old as time. It being a noble profession, the root of gossip is Gospel. Considering it comes from the Good Book, let it be known the first gossips were Matthew, Mark, Luke, and John. And everybody gossips.

Jackie Collins tells me, "If not for that delicious girl talk, I'd never have a best-seller. I put a tape recorder on a luncheon table and it's my friends' affairs and things they do and see and hear that I write about. If not for them I wouldn't know about multiple orgasms. Thank God for gossip."

In 1989 I interviewed Frau Gertraude Junge in Munich. Frau Junge was gray haired, widowed, seventy-seven years old. She lived modestly in a one-room apartment on an unpretentious street. It was a lifetime away from her days as private secretary to Adolf Hitler. At one point during our four and a half hours together she said in excellent but accented English, "Hitler was very friendly. We had many pleasant evenings at the Berghof with guests like Heinrich Himmler. I was at all the dinners. Part of my duty was to give some gossip at the table and relax Hitler. The Führer loved gossip!"

I guess, let's face it, it's television, telephone, telecommunications, tell a friend. So if all God's creatures love gossip, I can cut a little slack for Jazzy, too. Even he wants to know who and what.

During normal hours other warm bodies are around to monitor the phones. But come Sundays or late at night, we're hooked into the Jazzy Answering Machine.

The almost worst was the day an upset Sylvester Stallone rang. He'd called a few days earlier and given me a story. He'd been filming at Rahway Prison, a maximum-security facility in New Jersey. He'd said, "This is the most difficult prison in the world. The worst. I'm doing scenes with Cuban boat people, playing football with guys who've murdered six people apiece. The things they shout you can't believe . . . and they're all innocent. Some guy with a really hard look, like James Woods in *The Onion Field*, a guy who maybe killed five times, been arrested thirty-seven times, this guy swears he was framed . . . he's taking the rap for his brother. Every single one says that. Nobody in the whole joint is guilty."

I print this. That same day I get word Stallone is wild. Hysterical. I've put his life in jeopardy. He must speak with me. My assistant, Marcee, who has been with Joey and me for forty years and could find me on a sand dune in the Sahara, is tracking me down. Urgent. Urgent.

As I walk into my house, anguished Sylvester's on the phone screaming. His voice is actually so high only my dog can hear it. He hollers at me, "I'm going to get killed here, thanks to you."

"Excuse me?"

"You've created a goddamned riot."

My dog has selected this moment to bound onto my lap and bark in my ear.

"Will you stop that!" I cry out, trying to shake free of Jazzy.

"I should stop?" screams Stallone.

"No, not *you*, Sylvester."

"You're the one who should stop."

"Sorry, I didn't hear . . . what did you say?" I say into the phone while pushing my dog away.

"What the hell's the matter with you? How can you not hear? I'm at the top of my lungs!" shrieks Sly.

My dog now has clamped his teeth around my skirt and is tearing at it. Nazalene, who runs my home, appears in the doorway and I look at her, searching for answers as to why Jazzy is so wound up. Meanwhile, I speak into the phone. "What's wrong? What happened?"

"Nothing happened," Nazalene replies. "It's just that he gets wild when you get a call."

"What *happened*?! The prisoners are rioting as a result of what you wrote," Sly barks. "That's what happened."

"Listen, I can't deal with that right now," I whisper to Nazalene across the mouthpiece, which my animal is now trying to lick.

"What the hell do you mean, you can't deal with it now?" shouts Stallone. "You suggesting I should maybe get killed? You've hurt the feelings of everybody up here and the whole prison is up in arms and . . ."

Jazzy was fighting me for the receiver, which must've smelled from the chicken I'd had earlier, so I babbled to him, "Okay . . . okay . . . okay," while continuing the conversation with Sly.

"Okay, I got it," I say to him. "So what do you want me to do?"

"I think you should ask the trainer to deal with this telephone problem," said Nazalene, trying to pull a loudly barking Jazzy off my ear.

"Write another column for tomorrow and fix it up," crackles the line. "Say they're really good guys. It's costing me a hundred thousand dollars a day. It's thirty-two hundred dollars every minute I film. And because of you everything's ground to a total standstill."

"Yes, right, Sylvester."

Nazalene, who couldn't hear over the barking, was back at my elbow with, "The trainer's name is Ivan. Who's Sylvester?"

"What it's costing me I could've built a whole Stallone wing. Write good things about them fast. Jeez, say how terrific they've been. Say the prisoners are the best extras I've ever worked with. Say any friggin' thing you can think of that's positive."

"Stallone, Stallone," I bark back to Nazalene over my dog's barking.

"What? What? F'r crissakes," responds the receiver in my ear.

"I'm not talking to *you*, Sly."

"Why, you got something else going on right now that's more important? Somebody else you know is about to get killed?"

"He wants attention," said Nazalene as Jazzy earnestly addressed himself to licking my ear, the one that was attached to the telephone.

The next day I wrote another column about what sweet cons they had up in Rahway. I saved Sly's life.

I thought, Wouldn't it be great if I could only save mine?

Police have informants and columnists have sources. There are constant bulletins of breathless sightings. People ring excitedly from restaurant rest rooms to announce they've spotted a real live "Somebody" sucking juice out of some escargot somewhere. Muffled voices who you know are hiding their faces whisper hoarsely into the mouthpiece, "I'm at Nobu. Robert De Niro is across the way. He's eating."

Wow-ee! Stop the presses!

Writing a column is seductive. It gives access and power, but it takes its toll. Everyone wants. Everyone needs. Everyone calls. And the publicity junkies are always around. Mention them on Tuesday and they're back Thursday (providing Wednesday is a holiday). That means phone calls coming in. Lots of phone calls.

After one particularly long day that began with Chuck Norris at breakfast and was continuing straight through nonstop, I came into my home as the office phone was ringing. Gina Lollobrigida. Minutes into the conversation, the City Desk called to say there was a rumor about Streisand announcing another return tour (the woman's made more comebacks than Clinton) and could I check it out.

I'd disconnected Gina so I rang her back. She said, "Hello," and the paper called again. They had an anonymous tipster on the line who wanted to inform me that Cher was having as her houseguest her long-ago flame, the bagel maker Rob Camiletti. Cher had face-lifts older than this guy and the "tip" turned out to be bogus, but they needed to tell me and I needed to follow through. I hung up on Gina.

Then in came a collect call from Indonesia. My godchild, Karina Sukarno, daughter of Indonesia's first president and his Japanese wife, Dewi. Her half sister, Megawati, the current president of the country, was available to talk to me but couldn't do it on this particular connection, so could I hang up and call Megawati on another line?

I was just hunting for the number when, by happenstance, her mother called. Dewi was in Tokyo, I was in New York, Zubin Mehta was having an upcoming concert in Djakarta, and she wanted to invite him to her party and did I have his number?

Gina called again. I put Dewi on hold, and the City Desk checked in on the third line to inquire what did I learn about Streisand. At which point in came the one call I'd been waiting for. I'd been waiting for it for six months. It was from El Jefe. Manuel Antonio Noriega, onetime strongman of Panama. General Noriega's residence the past dozen years has been a jail cell in Miami.

I knew the general in his glory days. Our first interview in Panama City had been in May 1988 when he told me, "I do not fear Uncle Sam. I have absolutely no fear. And I am never nervous. I will go down fighting. I am not going anywhere. I have no intention of leaving this country. I do not say that Panama will not survive without Noriega. I say only that Noriega will not survive without Panama."

Shortly before our meeting, the elder President Bush's secretary of state, George Shultz, announced that his deal with Noriega had collapsed and that those drug indictments were back on. But that evening you couldn't tell it from Noriega, who smiled, sipped scotch, and worked the reception room party inside his National Security Council office.

He introduced one person to me with, "He does business with the United States."

I replied, "Your indictments, General, indicate you, too, have done business with the United States."

He answered in halting English, "My only business with the United States has been supplying information."

I'd interviewed him several times in Panama City. His daughters Sandra and Thays had visited me in New York and I them in Miami. We'd kept continuous communication by phone, letter, and fax dozens of times. I was in the courtroom when the general was sentenced as a war criminal. I was in contact with his lawyer, Frank Rubino.

Now, having served more than one-third of his thirty-year sentence and having been denied parole, there was some talk about new evidence and a new trial. He sent word he wanted to speak with me. I sent word I would fly down for a face-to-face interview. His daughters and his lawyer were arranging the proper day.

It is not easy to fix such an appointment. Certain days he is allowed visitors, certain days, not. Meanwhile, he wanted to speak with me on the telephone.

You can't just call a prisoner who's behind bars. You can't just dial Noriega and get him on the other end. He must call you. And in most cases the inmate is obliged to place his call collect.

In any case, all was finally arranged. All was in readiness. El Jefe had my unlisted number. I was set for his call. The question was, when? Once I was out and came home to intense disappointment when I was handed a message that General Noriega had called.

I couldn't call him back. I could only wait.

I waited.

Finally there was that very special afternoon. His unmistakable voice with the thick Spanish accent said clearly, "Cindy, it is the general. Cindy, I so glad to speak you. I have very special to tell you. Here is what I want only you to know. I am . . ."

Click. Dial tone.

Jazzy had walked across the buttons on the phone. Jazzy had disconnected General Manuel Antonio Noriega.

For a second, what flashed through my fevered brain was how lucky for us El Jefe was in jail. If this had been Noriega's old powerful glory days, my Jazzy could have ended up a dogsicle.

CHAPTER 18

Thanksgiving

Why the Pilgrims were thankful, I know. Who wouldn't want to get off that damn crowded ship? But for us non-Pilgrims, the best thing to give thanks for is that it's another 364 days until you have to assemble all your kinfolk together again.

There's the uncle who vacuums up all the dark meat. The brother-in-law who skims all the marshmallow off the sweet potato pie. Being locked in a room with a cousin whose entire career consists of borrowing money from you. It's not that we don't all love our families. It's just that it's all relative.

And the kids. God, those kids. My husband's nephew's

wife got pregnant because, she said, "We felt there might be something missing in our lives." Right. Privacy and sanity. She then changed her yowling infant's diaper just as I was ladling the gravy. I learned right then that the most important thing to know in rearing children is how to protect yourself.

That's why I loved to go away at Thanksgiving.

In his better years Joey and I always went away over Thanksgiving. The very last time my husband and I had been able to manage this was the year we went to Rio.

Rio, that glorious city where every girl from Ipanema appears to have legs that stretch right up to her brain, is also where every dinner starts at 11 P.M. Not such a great custom for Joey because by that hour he was already on seconds of Rolaids. The locals started perking up exactly as the Adamses started conking out.

The evening the American ambassador to Brazil was to give a party in our honor made Joey very happy because it would mean one dinner where he'd be served at a normal hour.

"Absolutely." The ambassador laughed.

We showed on the stroke of the appointed 8 P.M. Much later, when the invited guests had arrived, everyone was told, almost apologetically, that, because of the Guests of Honor, the food would be served early.

Promptly at midnight—I mean, at the stroke of twelve—dinner was served. This so exhausted Joey that the next day he was out flat at the Copacabana Hotel. He went to sleep at the pool. After schmearing suntan lotion all over, the man just prepared to sauté away. Rio's intense heat chemicalized the perspiration, and the oil and everything began running down his body. He reached over to a nearby table, found something to blot himself with, wiped the sweat from his face, around his neck, under his arms, in between the webs of his fingers, then he threw this sopping towel back on the table and once again zonked flat out.

The one other sunbather nearby bestirred himself to silently watch this exercise a moment, then plopped back in his beach chair. Minutes later Joey roused himself once more to mop his dripping body—up his nose, down his back, between his legs, inside his ears. Then, like before, he threw this rag back on the table. This time he half nodded to the other gentleman, who had raised himself up and was studying Joey's routine.

Instantly Joey fell into yet another snooze. The other man stood up, walked to the table, picked up Joey's sweaty rag, and put it on. It had been his shirt.

✲

Thanksgiving Day dawned snowy and bitterly cold, but I viewed even the five-hour drive upstate to Lake Placid Lodge as an adventure because I knew at the end of it there would be flowers in my cabin, a fleece robe on my bed, hot tea laid in front of my fireplace, handmade chocolates, heated towels, a bath with sea salts, and a game menu dinner.

I was excited.

The night before, my dog stopped eating. He wasn't feeling well. Diarrhea is not uncommon in little dogs who have teeny stomachs, but bloody diarrhea was something else. I was petrified. He was up the whole night, so I was up the whole night. Almost hourly he scampered off the bed and padded into the john. He has a doggy nook there as well as newspapers spread about for him. After I cleaned up after him, he dragged himself back to the bed. Then he returned to the john again. As the hours wore on, he wore down. I was scared. Facing a long drive and long weekend, I didn't know what to do.

My people were off. My vet was away over the holiday. I was all alone. The Animal Medical Center emergency room would probably have taken him from me for overnight observation, but I didn't want that. I felt so helpless. I took his gorgeous little face in my hands, but he couldn't tell me what he felt even though his tiny body was giving off major body language. The usually up, wagging tail was down and, if a dog can frown, he was. Nor was he cuddling. He lay atop the quilt at the foot of the bed, not snuggled under it with his body across me. And it was back and forth to the john.

I couldn't delay longer. At 5 A.M. I woke our vet, who was out of town. Dr. Kim said she'd talk me through this temporarily because she'd be in the office the next day. The problem was, I couldn't be there the next day. I would be in the Adirondacks, a day's journey away. Friends had spent weeks organizing this trip and, had I needed to cancel, it would have been an emotional hardship. Dr. Kim said give him Pepto-Bismol. I hung up and combed the city for a drugstore. Everything was closed. Eventually, I found Pepto-Bismol and, as I was ordered, tried crushing a tablet in his food. Lotsa luck. How about if he won't eat? So back out I went hunting Pepto-Bismol liquid and an eyedropper. But, then, how to get an eyedropperful down a cranky, wriggly Yorkie? Most of the pink liquid dried on his chin.

I was then told he was losing so much blood sugar I had to feed him honey. My house has Sweet'n Low—no jams, jellies, marmalade, or honey. Back out in the slush I trudged to hunt Golden Blossom. How to get *that* in him? Put it on your finger and massage it on his gums, Dr. Kim told me on our fifteenth call. Yeah? *You* try! I missed his mouth and schmeared it all over his whiskers, which were now gummy from honey. His face was pink, his whiskers stiff. Into the car we went.

I kept Jazzy in my lap all wrapped up in a warm blanket. I was in the backseat with my friend Arlene. An hour out, Jazzy whoopsed all over the backseat. While I wriggled around in that cramped space cleaning up the mess, Arlene held him. Jazzy repaid her kindness by doing a really dirty deed all over her. *All* over. Fortunately, Arlene was layered. Coat, outer sweater, inner sweater, T-shirt. We pulled off to the side of the road and off came her outer sweater.

Boyohboyohboy did we leave that thing there. We dug a hole in a snowbank and buried our fragrant paper towels, regular towels, plastic Baggies, wipes, newspapers, Kleenex, the whole gamut of tools we'd been working with. At a McDonald's we moistened napkins to wipe Jazzy clean. All the while we were on our cell phones and car phones talking to the vet.

Between my vet and the lodge manager Kathryn Kincannon's local vet, I was on the phone all weekend. Finally, finally, three days later Jazzy and I returned home. Two A.M. I awoke. Jazzy wasn't curled up beside me in bed. I ran to the bathroom to see a furry head and two paws flailing about in the john.

Jazzy had fallen into the toilet.

Happy Thanksgiving.

CHAPTER 19

Romeo and Jazzyet

F riends, suffused with the old song lyrics, "It's so nice to have a man around the house," had decided it was enough with my living alone. Their interest in hitching me up came right around the time I was doing a column on the rash of celebrity unions that had just gone poo. Bruce and Demi, Montel and Grace Williams, Meg Ryan and Dennis Quaid, Hank Azaria and Helen Hunt, the Gingriches, the Alan Thickes, the Harrison Fords, Mr. and Mrs. Mayor Rudy Giuliani, the four-times-married Ron Perelman and the third Mrs. Ron Perelman, Sumner and Phyllis Redstone, Roseanne and whoever, etc. The fact that I was content gave my friends no pleasure. In their view I needed a relationship. As the first anniversary of Joey's death approached, they began trying to fix me up.

Sally Jessy Raphael invited me for a weekend at her country house upstate. A modest little place—six stories with a baronial staircase plus an elevator. We're talking fifty-four rooms in the main house, another twenty in the carriage house, another God knows how many in the barn, a dozen more in the caretaker's cottage. With acreage that reaches to Colorado. I took one look and the thought came that I needed to get myself a talk show.

Sally didn't mention that my visit was a setup. She'd nailed a ringer for me and had thus invited me and this dude up for an overnight. She swore her place was only an hour from the city. Right. If you're shot out of a cannon.

Anyway, she put together a small dinner party to cement the evening. The group included Beverly Sills and her family plus Marylou Whitney, the widow of society's superrich Cornelius "Sonny" Vanderbilt Whitney, with her new husband who is of even more recent vintage than her inlays. Considering this was a casual winter evening in the rural pastoral countryside, Marylou wore only diamond teardrop earrings, diamond lavaliere necklace, diamond bracelet, diamond tiara, and a new 22-carat diamond solitaire surrounded by assorted diamonds—so it shouldn't just look like what you throw on to go to the supermarket to squeeze the bananas.

Another guest was movie critic Rex Reed, who arrived two hours and fifteen minutes late for dinner. Since he has a home twenty minutes away, it was hard to understand when he explained, "The directions were all wrong. I got lost. I left my house at five." It was now 9:15. So, Rex, why didn't you call from the car? "I have no car phone." So, Rex, why didn't you use your cell? "I have no cell." So, Rex, you got a quarter for a pay phone?

Seated next to me was a tall, good-looking, charming blond gentleman in a turquoise Chinese silk smoking jacket. Paul, I learned, was a composer. Talented. Well-to-do. With very fine bloodlines. Home was Oklahoma.

Over the salad course I asked Paul, "How long do you know my friend Sally Jessy Raphael?"

"We just met," he said pleasantly.

"Oh? Where?"

"Well, I'm visiting the city now and staying with friends. I went shopping on Madison Avenue the other day. There's a department store called Shanghai Tang."

"I know it well. Its original shop is in Hong Kong and it sells Chinese silk items much like what you have on."

"That is where I picked it up," he beamed. "It's where I also met Sally, who was shopping there at the same time."

"So you picked up Sally as well as the shirt?"

"No. Actually, she sort of picked me up. We were looking at things, just the two of us in the same department, and we struck up a friendly conversation. She asked what I did. I told her. She asked me if I was married. I told her no. So she said she had a friend she wanted me to meet and would I please come to dinner this weekend."

"So Shanghai Tang specializes in Chinese silks *and* unattached men."

Paul smiled appreciatively. He was quite nice, but for my future intended he lived too far away. Oklahoma's a tough daily commute.

Another time a friend arranged a blind date for me. I went along because, no matter what, it would make a great column. It was prearranged that we'd meet at Tavern on the Green. Very elegant.

I was dressed to the eyeballs. Not because I thought this was to be the future love of my life, but because that's what I do. Dress to the eyeballs. I think my birth certificate was written on a bugle bead. That night I sported more shiny accessories than a rock and roller's limo. Put it this way, I would have been overdressed for the Oscars.

In came my beauty. It was a chilly night.

Ready? No tie. No jacket. Short-sleeved shirt. The color was orange. Worn outside his trousers. We were a perfect made-in-heaven match. Like maybe the queen of England with Eminem. The restaurant manager took one look and whispered to me, "How quickly do you want the service?" I took another peek and whispered back, "Very."

The truth is, I do not want another relationship. I have a male in my life who sleeps with me, who doesn't argue about whether or not I like his family, who cuddles and snuggles, and who couldn't care less if I get fat or old or don't wax my chin.

He's taken the place of that one other special creature who had filled my home and heart for a lifetime. A bona fide member of my household, Jazzy leaches from my bones all the love that I now have no one to give. I don't just love this dog. I am *in love* with this dog. In my will I would leave my apartment to him if I thought he could handle the maintenance.

With that love comes all the coloration of such a relationship. I fuss over him ceaselessly. One gray day I bought him a red patent leather collar studded with red rhinestones and a sterling silver ID tag complete with a matching leash. A punker with spiky green hair, earring, nose piercings, and a studded leather headband stopped me on the street to gaze at him.

"Man, that's about the most beautiful thing I ever saw," glowed the dude.

I was so appreciative. Puffing with pride, I said, "Thank you. He's pure-blood from champion stock."

The guy blinked at me. "Yeah, the dog's nice, too, but I'm talking about his collar."

As with any other living creature on this planet, there is a price to pay for a relationship. To get back the nuzzling and smooshing I require, I must give what Jazzy requires. Not just what he needs. What he *wants*. Attention. Want to or not, I am forced to play with him.

There are periods when I am desperate to be all alone in the universe to contemplate the lint in my navel. But, no. He's barking, circling, yipping at my ankles, bringing me a ball to throw. I do not wish to pick up this ball. It's slimy. He's slobbered all over the thing. I also lack the energy and suppleness of limb to bend down and retrieve this stupid, icky, cruddy ball again and again.

If you crush him to your chest you can feel his tiny heart pumping. Lift him high over your head and your fingertips can count his little ribs. It's a wonder how such a small, inarticulate being can have an agenda. But he does. It's take care of Me, pay attention to Me, play with Me.

Arlene Dahl and her husband, Marc Rosen, also had a prospect laid on for my future and lured both this suspect and me to a sit-down at their weekend place upstate. It was okay to bring Jazzy because he'd frolic outside with their miniature schnauzer, Hansel.

This being Hansel's home and the guest list being a sort of Hollywood-on-the-Hudson, Hansel was quintessential perfect refinement. Jazzy, however, was not cohosting this party, so he therefore elected to fall into a deep, wet mud hole.

My charge came careening into the elegant dining room like a drowned rat, caked in slime and ooze. Wet, shivering, and scared, he came sliding in for his mommy to fix him and help him. Someone ran to the kitchen to get a towel. As I reached down to dry him, he gave himself a vigorous shake.

Unfortunately, what he shook was mud and ooze and slime and brown water all over drop-dead-gorgeous Joan Collins, who was pristine in sanitized, purified, glorified, dandified, all-over spotless beige silk. Or at least she had been. Through perfect teeth, the bitch from *Dynasty* bit off the words: "I . . . am . . . not . . . a . . . dog . . . person."

Right.

Needless to say, my date was not charmed.

My next setup came on a particularly trying day. I was to tape a TV interview with Raquel Welch. She had demands. She'd requested a limo. She was only a few blocks away, but fine. Wanted her own hairdresser and makeup person. Fine. Wanted only an afternoon taping. Fine. Wouldn't be interviewed at home or in her office. Fine. Forwarded lighting and camera instructions like lens filters, like favor the right side of her face, like a white silk screen placed out of camera range to bounce light off her so you can't see any dark lines. Fine.

Mind you, this was a news program, and news shows are more accustomed to photographing dead bodies and car crashes. They once photographed me up against a urinal because it was their only white wall. We're not talking sophisticated moviemaking here. We're not talking redoing *Gone With the Wind.* We're talking a four-minute Q&A with Raquel to push her new fitness video.

She arrived looking undeniably stunning, and the crew, who've shot everyone who ever lived except maybe Mme. Curie, muttered, "God, she's so uptight!" She was displeased with her chair, with her image on the monitor, with everything.

A few weeks before I'd had dinner with the actor Robert Wagner. R.J., as everyone calls him, never says a bad word about anyone. If Hitler ever came back, R.J. would say, "He's the best in his line." Robert Wagner just simply does not knock anyone. Except one person. Only one person did he even casually care to intimate was not the warmest, nicest, cuddliest human he'd ever met. That person was Raquel Welch.

So I said to her, "Why are you so difficult to work with?"

"Why ask me that?" she bristled. "Why not ask someone who's worked with me?"

"I did."

"Who?"

"Robert Wagner."

"And what did he say?"

"He said you're difficult to work with."

She unpinned her lapel mike, stood up, and lashed out at me, "And you're a barracuda." Then she stormed out.

I was supposed to go on the set live for that day's show. This whole experience had made me so nervous that my eyeballs dried up. Exactly as I sat down, adjusted my mike, smoothed my blouse, cleared my throat, and faced the camera, my right contact lens popped out. The thing actually separated from my eyeball as they zoomed in for a closeup. I looked like an outer-space alien. The camera was tight on my face as what looked like my pupil was rolling down my cheek.

The plan for me that night was to go out right from work, but because I needed to get another lens, I had to go home. I was covering a charity event in a public space downtown. My escort, the fix-up, and I were to dine at this pseudo-nightclub. He joined me in my apartment while I refreshed my contacts. And he went crazy for my dog.

He said, "I'm familiar with this place where we're going. They're used to dogs down there. Besides, the party planner is someone I know."

Since it was wintertime, I dressed Jazzy in the brand-new red mink coat with gold buttons that QVC furrier Dennis Basso had just made for him. "You sure we can take him?" I asked.

"No problem. I know just how to handle it," he said. "I love dogs. I've always had dogs. I know just how to handle these types of things. Leave it to me."

I left it to him. As we arrived at our table, my dog, whom nobody had realized we had with us at that point, crawled out of my date's pocket and knocked over the minicandle that was burning in the center of the table. Both of us plus two passersby and the waiter assigned to our station grabbed whatever was available hurriedly to tamp out the flame. We were stomping, we were stamping, Jazzy was barking.

Our machinations burned a big hole in the tablecloth

and singed a pile of napkins. The party planner, who was my escort's friend or, at least, used to be his friend, glared at us as we left—carrying the dog.

Humanly speaking, I think I'm destined to a life of singlehood.

CHAPTER 20

Big Women, Little Dogs

I n many households little doggies have taken the place of other partners. Thanks to technology, husbands are becoming obsolete. Today there are sex toys and devices, although I am reliably informed that the church frowns on jumper cables. Today a woman doesn't need a legal spouse. She doesn't even need a temp. She just puts her arms around a Bunsen burner, snuggles up to a warm latex glove, puts down her credit card, and she and her dish make a baby.

I've noticed another phenomenon that is possibly related. What the psychological view is, I don't know. I only know it appears that strong women are wild mad crazy insane for their teeny dogs. Do these bits of fluff replace husbands in the hearts of these women? In some cases, yes. Do they consume these otherwise hard-as-nails women with the gooshiest love? Absolutely.

Elizabeth Taylor Hilton Wilding Todd Fisher Burton Burton Warner Fortensky WhoKnowsWhatNext has been married so often she has rice marks on her face. Wash-and-wear wedding gowns. The woman's marriage licenses are on Xerox paper. Yet there remains in this lady's life one constant love: her white Maltese, Sugar. Sugar has warmed Elizabeth's bed longer than any of those two-legged household pets who've romped on her mattresses.

Joan Rivers. Wonderful, marvelous lady. But ever to be mistaken for Mother Teresa, I don't think so. Joan's beloved Spike, now deceased, used to sprawl across a mink blanket that was spread in front of his mommy's log-burning fireplace. Figuring in dog years, Spike lived longer than Dick Clark. Even today, if you talk to Joan about Spike, she starts to cry. She says, "Please. I don't want to think of it. I don't know how I was able to survive."

Judge Judy. One evening Judy called to cancel a date we'd made for dinner. "Can't do it," she said in her trademark clipped fashion. "Can't go out for dinner. I can't leave Lulu."

"Who's Lulu?"

"What do you mean, who's Lulu? Lulu is my life. The center of my being."

"Okay, so bring her along."

"She doesn't want to go. She's hiding in a corner."

"Excuse me? Who is this bitch?"

"A very spoiled bitch. My shih tzu."

Her Honor's shih tzu is the size of a pot roast. TV's tough love judge, who easily sentences humans to fines, miseries, unhappy rulings, was so stricken at having to leave her animal alone that she canceled going to dinner. She ordered in takeout just so as not to leave Lulu.

Esquire's publisher, Valerie Salembier, a gourmet cook, had a busy weekend coming up. A dinner party she was preparing all herself. Chinese delicacies. For ten important guests. She felt so guilty about having no playtime for her dog that she sent him to a day-care center.

Shirley MacLaine, who can't bear for her pet to be alone, hires a sitter for him when they go to a strange city.

I went to a charity dinner. The hostess was an uptight socialite whose face had been lifted so often there's nothing left in her shoes. The belly button is now the nose. I think if she sneezed she'd blow her brains out. This night the newly uplifted face was hanging down. She was upset. Why? Her Pekingese didn't feel well.

One beauty capped her dog's teeth. Another's Rover was happiest driving in the back of her car. When the dog died, Madame buried him in the backseat of her Cadillac. The whole Caddy, Lhasa apso and all, was lowered into the ground.

I have personal knowledge of a cheapo socialite who gave her husband a minimalist funeral and spent limited money when her father went to his reward, but ordered the most expensive price-is-no-object doggy coffin when her terrier died.

I know a powerful district leader for the Republican party. The problem is, although people line up to see her, she rarely wants to go out because of her four-pound toy poodle. Sara has white fur, black eyes, and separation anxiety. "I can't bear leaving Sara alone," says the GOP's big-time district leader.

This is normal? Maybe not to you. Maybe yes to Cheryl Tiegs, whose staffers have flown coach while her fox terriers, Martini and Olive, enjoyed the superclass luxury of an MGM Grand. Maybe yes to Lily Tomlin, who'd speak baby talk to her Norwich terrier, Tess. Who'd rehearse her act in front of Tess. Who'd dress Tess as Baby Jesus for the front of her Christmas card. Maybe yes to bichon frise owner Kathie Lee Gifford, who says of her pets' trainer, "Too bad he isn't a marriage counselor. If only he could do for husbands what he does for dogs."

Apparently the concept is that a ferocious exterior protects an insecure interior. Dr. Ellen Siroka, a psychologist for people, says, "Strong women are always concerned about letting their guard down. They can be tough on their men, too. Caring for a tiny creature who is totally dependent on them for food and shelter is the only way they can let their vulnerability out. Little dogs are touchy-feely. You can fondle them, cuddle in bed, hold them in your lap."

The world has seen the queen of England's corgis and her nemesis the late Duchess of Windsor's pugs. It hasn't, however, seen Mariah Carey playing *boinggggg* with her Jack Russell. Tossing a ball in the air for him to bounce on his nose. Performing for thousands at a concert, then entertaining an audience of one in her kitchen.

Great dames rarely have Great Danes. To them size does matter. Big hounds are aggressive by nature. When they mess up, it's a big mess. A lapdog has portability.

Charlene Nederlander is married to James Nederlander, who produced the hit musical *Rent*, who produced the hit drama *Copenhagen*, who's a serial Tony winner, who owns New York's Nederlander Theaters, the second most powerful theater chain on Broadway. Charlene and Jimmy have been married since the Stone Age. Charlene adores Jimmy. She cares for Jimmy, watches over him, monitors his food, his health, his disability. Charlene will say things like, "Oh, poor Jimmy, he had to go to the doctor today." Charlene will also say things like, "Oh, poor Emmy, I have to take her to the vet today." With her husband she sends an aide. With her Yorkie she goes personally.

Last winter we traveled through Europe together, and our train was stopped in the chunnel between London and Paris because the Parisian transportation workers were striking. Stalled, in a parlor car with lousy luncheon food, we ended up discussing our pets. So, does Charlene really spoil her Yorkie?

Jimmy, who had just bought his wife a string of black pearls, gave a one-syllable answer: "Uggggh!" Translation: "You nuts? She loves this hound more than me."

Leona Helmsley has a Maltese named Trouble. Trouble travels Mama's personal 727 to their Greenwich, Aspen, Sarasota, Manhattan homes. Traverses the city in Mama's chauffeured stretch. Shops Bergdorf's under Mama's arm. Even lunches on Mommy's lap at restaurants where dogs are not allowed.

There's the trust issue. The only living, breathing organism Leona is sure she can trust not to want her money or Rolodex is her dog. And can anyone see hauling a rottweiler into Bergdorf's or sneaking an Alsatian into a restaurant where ladies who lunch are lunching?

Jennifer Lopez's Raea, an even teenier chihuahua than the former Taco Bell spokespooch, travels cradled next to Jennifer's chest, although God knows where she hid when her mother sported that naked outfit at the Grammys. She even attends recording sessions snuggled into Jennifer, who says, "I need to hold her after each workout. She makes me feel calm."

The bigger the diva, the smaller the dog. Madonna wanted her chihuahua to be happy. Chiquita was so spoiled that she couldn't handle *any* separation. When Madonna's first baby came and this love had to be shared, the dog suffered an emotional breakdown. She had to be given months of training.

Madison Avenue jeweler Judith Ripka dearly loves her four-pound Pookie as much as her husband, who weighs considerably more. But she'll tell you flatout, "Look, I worship my husband, but don't ever ask me to choose."

There's Joanna Mastroianni. Sharon Stone and Jane Seymour wear Joanna creations. Joanna's Pomeranian, Natasha, has the run of her Sutton Place apartment. Also the run of her Seventh Avenue showroom. To a couturiere, a department store buyer is like what a large solitaire is to Ivana. Ain't nothing more important. So this one day, in comes a major buyer with a checkbook and a pencil. He's writing orders like crazy for a big-time big-spender specialty store in Houston. Sounds good, right? Not good. Natasha for some reason did not like this guy. And proved it. Right on top of his moccasin. This was not nifty for business since the buyer did not finish the order but left in a shot to find a shoeshine parlor.

Sighed Joanna, "Another buyer I can always get. What am I going to do, get rid of Natasha?"

There's Bette Midler and her adored Jack Russell, who goes by the name of Queen Puddles. There's Ingrid Rossellini and her dachshund, Yuma. There's Blaine Trump, who gets teary on the subject of her Yorkie. Jammed one night against Uma Thurman, Chevy Chase, and Barry Diller at Elaine's, she said to me, "I feed Pearl in between meals, which you shouldn't, but I do because I love her so much. Pearl runs the whole house. I revolve around Pearl."

With Mary Tyler Moore it's Shayna, whom Mary adopted from New Jersey Schnauzer Rescue. There's novelist Erica Jong's Godzuki, who even poses in ads with her. And Mary J. Blige, who tells me she's taking some of her recording royalties and redoing one room "because Popeye, my Pekingese, has just destroyed her special corner."

What is the explanation for such passion? Is it that career-driven women have a feminine side that yearns to give nurturing love and receive, in turn, unconditional love?

Is it that strong women resent that they are forced to be competitive? That they realize a man can leave them but a Westie won't? That a dog is the substitution for love?

Is it that we need something soft and cuddly? Some living, breathing organism that exists only for us and that generates love without judgment?

Right after his last book, his eighty millionth best-seller, Sidney Sheldon told me, "After my final book signing I'm taking my wife to Alaska." Yeah, why? "To see the aurora borealis." Yeah, why? "Because she's never seen it and because it's truly a phenomenon."

That's it, I thought. That's what this is. This unfathomable passion for a teeny-tiny skein of hair that's helpless, totally dependent on you, doesn't care if you smell bad, look bad, or act bad, is just as true as the aurora borealis. It's a real plain and simple phenomenon.

Whether this is why I phone from across the world

just to hear Jazzy bark, why I actually sniff his ears because I was told a bad odor right there is a sign of unwellness, why I take his temperature to be sure he's fine, why I massage his gums with my finger with a doggy toothpaste that tastes like peanut butter because I sense he won't floss by himself, why I cut up a brand-new maroon four-ply cashmere turtleneck to make a sweater for him, who the hell knows. I only know it's true love.

CHAPTER 21

Together Forever

One morning, Reggie announced, "Jazzy's turned into Joey."

My dog was minding his business, amusing himself quietly. Chewing some sort of skanky squeaky toy.

"He's living the same life as Joey. He's like Joey reincarnated."

I stared at my dog. "What are you talking about?"

"Look."

I looked. He was scrunched deep into a big overstuffed armchair.

"That was Joey's favorite spot."

He was right. But I was so accustomed to seeing Jazzy there that I never registered exactly where he was sitting.

"He's in the kitchen, right?"

"Yeah," I nodded. "Right."

"And where did Joey like to schmooze?"

"The kitchen."

"And how many places to plop are there in here? Two armchairs, a hassock, a banquette, six kitchen chairs, a couple of benches, and his own doggy bed. And where's Jazzy always sit?"

"In that one armchair."

"And where did Joey always sit?"

"In that one armchair."

Nazalene said, "Reggie and I talk about this often. Jazzy has become Joey."

Nazalene started to laugh. "Your husband only wanted to be where you were. As long as you were around and he could see you, he was happy. He would amuse himself. He would do his crossword puzzles. Play by himself, right?"

Now Reggie started to laugh. "Same with Jazzy. If you stay here he plays quietly. You go in another room he'll be nervous until you come back. When you're busy doing something, he'll rub his paws against your body until you put away what you're doing. Pick him up, hug him, and he'll stay in your arms forever. He'll almost purr.

"The point is, you created this. There's something you're doing that manufactures this. Maybe you have a need to cater, who knows. You always kissed Joey's face. Sometimes his eyes, his ears. You do the same with Jazzy. You've basically replicated what you've always done with the one creature in your life. I've seen you put your dog's whole ear in your mouth."

"Yes. It's so."

"And does he like it?"

"Well, let's put it this way, he hasn't said he doesn't."

"If in fact you can't believe your dog is like your husband, at the very least you have to acknowledge he's developed similar habits."

Added Reggie, "And who did your house revolve around? And your schedule? Joey. You always had to be home in time for him. You always carried his favorite things along with you if you went anywhere. So now it revolves around Jazzy. Now you pack *his* things along with you."

Said Nazalene, "Take the temperature. Your husband always felt a chill. You know the thermostat in the house was always turned way up because of him."

Right. Never a time I wasn't dying of heat. It's the same with Jazzy. His little body shivers if there's a breeze. The result is I have perennially damp armpits. Always warm. I suffered that with Joey. I was now suffering that with Jazzy.

There was another thing I hadn't wanted to tell them for fear they'd pick on me. Joey would never go to sleep unless I went with him. It was always a hassle if I wanted to lie down early. He'd sulk if I knocked off before him. However, if he was set to say nighty-night, it made no difference whether I was ready or not. I had to go to bed. Same with Jazzy. He wouldn't crawl into his bed or onto mine unless I was there. And if I stayed under the covers until high noon, so would he. He'd never move.

If my dog was napping, I'd slink around softly so as not to wake him. It's what I did with my husband, who'd snooze in his favorite chair. One day I actually caught myself tiptoeing past Jazzy. I realized I'd lost it. I remember saying to myself, "Idiot. This is a dog. Not a husband." Still, I worried about disturbing him. Still, I tiptoed.

Another thing. While triple-A invitations came in to me from the White House and the UN, my evenings in Joey's late years were primarily relegated to second-string people because the first-level VIPs couldn't be bothered with anyone in his frail state. I became dependent on those who would be kind enough to direct conversation to him. I was doing the same now. Only instead of people who were partial to Joey, it was people who were partial to

Jazzy. I had made a change in name only. Before it was dinner dates. Now it was play dates.

We all three looked over at Jazzy. He was scratching himself vigorously. We all three looked at one another. We all three fell silent. We looked back at him. We looked back at one another. We looked back into the inner recesses of our minds.

Nazalene finally broke the silence. "Mr. Adams," she whispered in an awestruck voice.

All of us looked at this dog. He was again scratching himself vigorously.

Reggie, whose eyes were as wide as saucers, said very quietly, "Look, I don't know what to tell you. I myself don't know what to make of this. I know it's silly, but this is Joey. It's Joey come back to life."

"Oh, my God," said Nazalene, staring at Jazzy, who was scratching away.

In his last ten years, my husband had suffered from a chronic dry skin problem called neurodermatitis. He'd bleed from the dig of his nails. A Viennese bakery didn't have as many assorted creams as Joey did. Still he itched.

We all three stared at Jazzy. He was scratching. And itching.

Nazalene was in the habit of combing Jazzy and

brushing him several times a day. She'd done it in times gone by with Joey, whose head also itched.

Where was Shirley MacLaine when you needed her? This was reincarnation. My husband the dog.

In Joey's time, if I had an important appointment and it was raining, I'd have to fend for myself because the car was waiting. Just sitting there with Reggie in it, waiting for Joey—in case. In case he wanted to go to lunch. In case we needed to send it for a doctor. Always in case.

"Well," I said to Reggie, "at least I still have *you* to myself. At least I don't have to worry this dog is going to take my car and driver."

Later that day I was off to see Patti LaBelle, who was doing a concert in town. I was told I couldn't be late because she was on a tight schedule. Since the interview was around the hour I usually played with this new male in my life, I put my hound in the backseat in order to have a twenty-minute cuddle en route to Patti's hotel. This way we had our fun time and I still wasn't late for the appointment.

The strong fragrance emanating from Patti's suite nearly reached the lobby. It wasn't perfume. It wasn't flowers. I couldn't believe it, but it was almost like I was smelling liver and onions.

Damn, it *was* liver and onions. "Girl," said Patti, grinning, "I cook my ass off in this room. I have all my pots hidden. The other day I made sautéed salmon, snow peas with lots of garlic, and the people who work here, they smelled it and came on in.

"See, honey, I carry my own kitchen. Hot plate, electric stove, frying pan, two-burner stove, Teflon pots.

"A dinky little crappy room service hamburger with fries costs me twenty-five dollars. I hate to throw money away and I like to *see* my food. I mean, that room service shit is not like down-home food.

"Last night I made okra, fresh corn on the cob, jumbo shrimp that we got from the market with onions, garlic, oregano, green pepper, and fresh tomato in oil.

"Hotels send up shit and you've got to pay fortunes for it. Girl, I've been performing twenty-five years. If I don't end up with money I'll get my head examined. At home I live a plain life. I clean, I dust, I'm out there with the mop. I cook because I'm always ready to eat. Last night I ate chicken backstage. During a costume change. Each time I came out I had chicken in my teeth."

It was a good interview. Great quotes. It was snowing when I hit the street. I saw all the poor souls scurrying for cover, opening umbrellas, desperately trying to flag cabs. As I looked for Reggie and my car I was feeling pretty impressed with myself. Not only did I get a good story but, yeah, okay, so Patti sure lived the good life but, you know what, so did I.

Fifteen minutes later still no Reggie. I phoned the car. "I'm finished. I'm on the street. Where are you?" I asked.

Silence for a minute, then, "I'm way across town. Don't you remember?"

"Remember what?"

"Jazzy needed the car. I had to take him for his play date."

A FINAL WORD

Joey. Jazzy. An original love story.

And as the sun sets on the horizon, it's Jazzy and me . . . barking happily ever after. . . .